Focus on Grammar

TEACHER'S MANUAL

A
BASIC
Course for
Reference
and Practice

Focus on Grammar

TEACHER'S MANUAL

A
BASIC
Course for
Reference
and Practice

Irene E. Schoenberg

Addison-Wesley Publishing Company
Reading, Massachusetts • Menlo Park, California
New York • Don Mills, Ontario • Wokingham, England
Amsterdam • Bonn • Sydney • Singapore • Tokyo
Madrid • San Juan • Paris • Seoul, Korea • Milan
Mexico City • Taipei, Taiwan

Focus on Grammar: A Basic Course for
Reference and Practice, Teacher's Manual

Editorial Director: Joanne Dresner
Development Editor: Joan Saslow
Production Editorial: Carol Harwood
Text Design Adaptation: Curt Belshe
Cover Design: A Good Thing, Inc.

ISBN 0-201-65682-5

2 3 4 5 6 7 8 9 10-VG-9897969594

Contents

Introduction

Focus on Grammar: A Basic Course for Reference and Practice helps beginning and intermediate students of English not only to understand and practice basic English grammar, but to use it with confidence. This Teacher's Manual suggests ways to use and enrich the material in the book. The first section contains general suggestions for teaching every unit. The second section gives practical teaching suggestions and culture notes to accompany specific exercises in the book. The third section is a tapescript of the listening activities in the Student Book. The listening activities feature comprehension checks and tasks, and clozes. The final listening from Appendix 20 demonstrates pronunciation of the phonetic alphabet. A complete answer key to the Diagnostic and Final Tests precedes the ready-to-use Diagnostic and Final tests.

Focus on Grammar is based on the assumption that a combination of activities leads to the effective use of English grammar. The emphasis you give to each type of activity should reflect the background, personality, and aims of your students. Among language learners there are two distinct types: the "scientists" and the "gamblers." While the scientists need to study, read, and practice specific points before they gain the confidence to interact communicatively, the gamblers are comfortable using whatever ability they have in the language and communicate from the start. Generally the danger among the scientists is that they confuse knowing about grammar and being able to do controlled activities with knowing the language. These individuals need more work with the communication practice exercises. The gamblers, on the other hand, often can communicate with ease and fluency, but when they neglect to focus on form and grammatical accuracy, their language becomes frozen at a certain level.

Using *Focus on Grammar*, you can offer your class a comfortable balance for the scientists, the gamblers, and those who are a combination of both.

General Suggestions

INTRODUCTORY CONVERSATION

Students listen and read theme-based conversations that contextualize the grammar of the unit, enabling them to hear and see each structure in a realistic situation. Here are ways you can engage students in the conversation.

Preview the dialogue: Before students listen to or read the conversation, spark their interest by giving background information about the characters in the conversation, asking about the illustrations, personalizing the material, and providing cultural information. See the second section of this Teacher's Manual for specific suggestions and cultural notes for all the introductory conversations in the book. After you preview the material, either play the cassette or read the dialogue aloud so students may hear it. After students hear the dialogue, you may wish to have them read it.

Vocabulary practice: More difficult vocabulary words are highlighted in a box. You may wish to discuss these words just before or after reading the conversation. Sometimes when you draw a picture or give an example from real life, it helps students to remember the word. In addition, it is generally a good idea to relate vocabulary words to students' lives.

For example, Unit 1 contains the following words and phrases: *daughter, detective, worried, I'll do my best, she's in love.* You may wish to draw a family tree showing a mother, a father, and a daughter to illustrate the meaning of the word *daughter,* or you may wish to show a picture of a famous mother and her daughter (Queen Elizabeth and Princess Anne, for example). You can draw a girl with hearts above her to show *she's in love.* For *detective,* mention famous detectives like Sherlock Holmes. Show a worried face and a happy face to help explain *worried.* Also, whenever possible, personalize the vocabulary to help students remember it:

> *Are you a daughter?*
>
> *Are you a detective? Is _____* (name another student) *a detective?*
>
> *Are you worried about your English? Is _____* (name another student) *worried about his English?* (If a student says, "I don't know," tell him or her to ask the other student.)
>
> *Are you in love?* (Be careful whom you ask!)

The boxed vocabulary items appear in their base form except for the idioms in Unit 1. The vocabulary items are presented in the following order: nouns, adjectives, verbs, prepositions, adverbs, and idioms. Vocabulary from the introductory dialogues is listed in order of appearance.

Comprehension: These questions check students' understanding of the conversation. After students have worked alone, ask them to compare their answers with a classmate's. Walk around the room and make certain the students are answering correctly. Go over the answers as a class. "That's wrong" answers refer to statements that contradict what is in the conversation, while "I don't know" answers are for those that are just not mentioned. The "I don't know" option acts as a springboard to conversation and encourages students to read the dialogue more carefully. Discuss and personalize the material when possible. For example, after answering a question that asks if Pete and Elenore are hungry or thirsty, ask students in class if they are hungry or thirsty.

After you have gone over the questions and answers, play the cassette again. First have students listen. Then have them listen and read. Beginners and intermediate students need to hear as much as possible of natural language that is tailored to their levels.

Practice with a partner: When you feel certain that the students understand the conversation, ask them to practice it with a partner. Encourage them to mimic the tape and exaggerate their part. From time to time ask one or two sets of students to perform the conversation for the class.

GRAMMAR CHARTS AND GRAMMAR NOTES

The grammar presented in *Focus on Grammar* reflects the spoken English of the United States and Canada. More formal usage is mentioned in the Grammar Notes, but the aim here is to get students comfortable with the spoken form. Throughout the book, contractions, short answers, *who* when referring to an object, *will* with *I* and *you, not as . . . as,* and the ordinal number with written addresses are practiced and used, since this is the spoken English of daily life.

Grammatical terms are used throughout the book. Though students are not asked to produce these terms, they are helped to understand them. Since most intermediate and advanced books use the terms and many students have encountered them in their own language, it seems beneficial to include them here, especially since *Focus on Grammar* can later be used by students as their grammar reference.

Before you refer students to the grammar charts and notes, if you happen to know a popular or folk song that uses the grammar you are about to present, write the lyrics on the blackboard. Sing for your class and then with them. It's a nonthreatening and enjoyable way to introduce a grammar point, even if you are not a Sills or Pavarotti.

You may approach the grammar presented in the charts and notes deductively or inductively. When teaching deductively, you read the notes with the class, refer to the charts, and make sure the class understands the notes. By asking the class to give additional examples to illustrate each note, you can check students' understanding.

A deductive presentation should take place before doing the exercises. Certain structures are more amenable to a deductive approach, and certain learners are more satisfied and successful with this approach to grammar. Indeed, when a grammar note is very simple and mostly a matter of form or when a grammar rule is extremely complicated to explain, a deductive approach is probably best for basic-level students. Also, when students have too little language to be able to state a rule or explanation, a deductive presentation is best. When the rule is simple, getting students to analyze and synthesize it may be too time-consuming and take away from time spent practicing the grammar.

Although it takes more time to get students to discover the rule inductively, in some instances for some learners it is beneficial because it involves the student as an active participant. This method is generally better for students who have had some exposure to the language. The second part of this Teacher's Manual gives examples of teaching grammar points inductively. (See pages 6 and 7.) It also provides additional specific information about the grammar charts and notes.

FOCUSED PRACTICE EXERCISES

These exercises give students a chance to practice the material described in the preceding section. There are objective answers to each question, so the exercises can be done alone as self-study or in class. In class, students can work in pairs, helping one another and seeking to understand the grammar. When students do Focused Practice exercises together, encourage them to think about the material rather than just produce the right answer. As students go over an exercise, you can make the material more relevant by pointing out the grammar rule and personalizing the material. Because so many exercises are contextualized, a great deal of incidental learning takes place while students are practicing the grammar. If a class is particularly strong in its knowledge of grammar but weak in communicative skills, you may wish to assign the Focused Practice exercises for homework and independent study and spend class time on the Communication Practice exercises.

COMMUNICATION PRACTICE EXERCISES

While these exercise take up little space in the book, they provide students with opportunities to expand all their language skills, and they often take up more class time than all the other activities combined. Since it is harder to control the time and direction of communication practice, and since these exercises require that students take responsibility for what they learn, it is important for you to help your students see the benefit of this type of practice. Students need to be weaned from the traditional notion that in class the teacher stands up and lectures while the students take notes and repeat what they have heard. Sometimes it takes a while before students realize how much they can learn from open-ended, interactive activities. You can help students get involved in the material in several ways: (1) Go around from group to group. Listen and respond to students' remarks. Encourage them to say more. (2) Involve students with their classmates. Ask questions: *Do you agree with Juan? What do you think?* or *How about you?* (3) When group work is concluded, ask for the groups' results and compare them with other groups. The rewards of interacting meaningfully in a target language for the basic-level student is very exciting and leads to a great deal of satisfaction.The more students feel that what they say is important, the more they are encouraged to use language daringly, creatively, and accurately.

REVIEW OR SELFTESTS

The Review or SelfTests give students a chance to check their knowledge of the unit's grammar and review any weaknesses before taking the final test. It is encouraging to do well on tests. By providing a practice test, students who prepare can achieve good results.

Teaching Suggestions and Culture Notes

This section contains specific suggestions for the material in *Focus on Grammar: A Basic Course for Reference and Practice*.

Starred items are for more advanced students or groups (see, for example, page 6).

Meet Your Class

A   Names and Countries (page 2)

Culture note: In informal situations it is common for Americans and English-speaking Canadians to use first names when speaking to acquaintances and co-workers. In more formal situations, a title (*Mr., Ms., Dr. etc.*) is used before a family (last) name. In cases of uncertainty, the older person or person with higher status decides whether to use first or last names.

Further practice: To help your new students become acquainted with each other, ask them to practice the conversation with a partner. Tell your students to change *James Belmont, Lucille Winston*, and *Vancouver, Canada* to their names and countries.

B   The Alphabet (page 3)

Culture note: In Canada, the last letter of the alphabet, *z*, is pronounced "zed."

Expansion: You may wish to give the students more practice with the alphabet. Ask a student to write on the chalkboard. You call out letters. The student writes the letters on the board while the other students write the letters in their notebooks. (Students usually have most difficulty with the vowels and the letters *j, g, w, x, z*). Or spell a word or words (*c-o-u-n-t-r-y, t-h-e U-n-i-t-e-d S-t-a-t-e-s*). A student writes the word or words on the chalkboard. Students in their seats call out the word or words. At this time you may want to spell your name and then introduce yourself to the class: *My name is Katherine Jones. Please call me Ms. Jones.*

OR *Please call me Katherine.*

OR *Everyone calls me Kate.*

C   Your Classmates (page 3)

Introductions: Ask students to introduce themselves to the class. (*My name is _____ . Please call me _____ .*)

Expansion: Bring in a large world map.

A student goes to the map. First the teacher, then other students ask, *Where's _____ ?* The student points to it on the map. The teacher points to places on the map and asks, "*Who's from _____ ?*" The class calls out the student's name.

UNIT 1

INTRODUCTION

THE MYSTERY OF ROCKY (page 4)

PREVIEW THE DIALOGUE.

Background and culture note: Before students listen to or read the conversation, you may wish to say, *Carol is a student in Oregon. Her family is in New York. Many students in the United States go to colleges far from home.*

Personalization: Familiarize students with characters and personalize the material. Pete is worried about his daughter. She is in Oregon. He is in New York. Pete is far from Carol. Ask students: *Where is your family? Are you worried about your family? Is your family worried about you? Are you far from your family? Are you homesick?*

After students have listened to and read the conversation, ask them:

Are you a detective? Who's a detective in the story? Are you a businessman? (If yes, How's business?) Who's a businessman? Are you a teacher? Who's a teacher? Are you a student? Are you in Oregon? Are you in New York?

Optional role play: Talking on the telephone.

A: Hello.
B: Hi _____ ? (Give your partner's name.)

A: Yes.
B: This is _____ . (Give your name.)

A: Hello, _____ . (Give your partner's name.) How are you? How's school?
B: I'm fine, and school is great.

GRAMMAR

A Affirmative Statements with *Be* (page 6)

Some groups may benefit from an inductive approach to the grammar.

Before reading the Grammar Notes, ask the class for sentences about students and things in the class using the verb *be*. Write them on the chalkboard. (Examples: *Maria is from Colombia. Pierre and Rene are from France. Hiro and Yoshimi are from Japan. The book is big. The dictionaries are open.*)

Point out the grammar labels. Tell students that *Maria, Pierre, Rene, Hiro* and *Yoshimi* are subject nouns; *is, am, are* are verbs; *from Japan* is a prepositional phrase; *a student* is a noun; and *big* and *open* are adjectives. Ask students what words can replace *Maria* and *Pierre and Rene*?

Tell students that *she, they, we, I,* and *it* are pronouns. Ask students to give a rule about the relationship between subject nouns and subject pronouns. (Subject pronouns can replace subject nouns.)

Ask students how many forms there are of *be* in the present. (three)

Ask students what grammatical features can follow the verb *be*? (nouns, adjectives, and prepositional phrases)

Then ask students to open their books and read the Grammar Notes together.

B Contractions of Affirmative Statements with *Be* (page 8)

Punctuation notes: Show the placement of the apostrophe above the line. Ask students to tell you which letter is replaced by the apostrophe. At this time you may wish to mention that a period comes at the end of a statement and capital letters at the beginning.

C Negative Statements and Contractions with *Be* (page 10)

After reading the grammar notes, ask students to make negative statements about the class and students, such as *The dictionary isn't red. Pierre's not from Japan. Yuriko isn't in class.*

Some linguists say that in negative statements the contraction of the pronoun + *be* is more emphatic than the contraction of *be* + *not*

> More emphatic: **He's** not fat. (pronoun + *be* contraction)
>
> He **isn't** fat. (*be* + *not* contraction)

C. 5 (page 13)

 Expansion: Groups follow the model and write a similar exercise. (Ten sentences with *be* in which only two are always true.) The teacher corrects the sentences. Then one student reads the sentences aloud or writes them on the chalkboard. The other groups find the two sentences that are always true.

C.7 (page 14)

Culture notes: There are fifty states in the United States. Two states, Alaska and Hawaii, are separated from the other forty-eight states. Washington, D.C. is the capital of the United States. It is not a state; it is a federal district.

There are ten provinces in Canada. The capital of Canada is Ottawa. Canada is large in size (3,851,790 sq mi) but small in population (26 million people).

D *Yes/No* Questions and Short Answers (page 15)

Punctuation note: Show students where to put the question mark.

Pronunciation note: The voice rises at the end of *yes/no* questions.

Inductive approach: Before reading the Grammar Notes, ask students to give all possible answers for a *yes/no* question with *I* in the answer and all possible answers with another pronoun in the answer. Ask students how many answers there are for *yes/no* questions with *I* and for *yes/no* questions with other pronouns in both the affirmative and the negative.

Example:	four answers	five answers
Are you happy?	Yes.	No.
	Yes, I am.	No, I am not.
	Yes, I'm happy.	No, I'm not.
	Yes, I am happy.	No, I am not happy.
		No, I'm not happy.

	four answers	seven answers
Are they happy?	Yes.	No.
	Yes, they are.	No, they are not.
	Yes, they're happy.	No, they're not.
	Yes, they are happy.	No, they aren't.
		No, they're not happy.
		No, they aren't happy.
		No, they are not happy.

Point out that short answers with contractions are more informal and common than long answers and answers without contractions.

 Long answers without contractions are not common in speaking. They are mainly used for special emphasis.

D.4 (page 18)

Expansion: Ask *yes/no* questions about the occupations of famous people:

> *Is Dustin Hoffman an actor?*

E *It's* + Time (page 19)

Culture note: In the United States and Canada most people try to arrive on time for interviews, jobs, and dinner invitations. If a person cannot come on time, he or she should call, apologize, and explain why. People are more relaxed about the time of arrival at large parties and informal gatherings.

E.4 (page 21)

In exercises where there are no writing lines, you can decide whether to make the exercise an oral or written one. In general, the lower the level, the more helpful it is for students to write out answers.

E.5 (page 22)

Personalization: To practice time and point out differences in time zones, ask students the time in different countries.

Personalization:

Ask: *Who in this class is usually early, on time, late?*

Talk about watches: *My watch is from Japan. It's an old watch, but it's a very good watch. It's ten years old, but it's always on time.*

WRAP IT UP (PAGE 24)

Comprehension check: Make sure all students understand that Rocky is not a boyfriend, but a pet.

Ask students what's right: *Carol loves Rocky.*

OR *Carol is in love with Rocky.*

Then ask,

Why is Carol safe with Rocky?

Culture note: Dogs are popular pets in the United States and Canada. People also have cats, birds, and fish. Some people have unusual pets, like snakes and monkeys. Talk about pets: *Are dogs popular in your country? Are other animals popular?*

UNIT 2

INTRODUCTION

WONDERFUL SONS, LUCKY DAUGHTERS-IN-LAW (page 29)

PREVIEW THE DIALOGUE.

Explain and personalize family ties: To demonstrate what a mother-in-law is, draw a family tree. Point out the father, mother, son, daughter, grandchildren, daughter-in-law, son-in-law, mother-in-law, and father-in-law. Tell the class, *Lulu Winston is a mother-in-law. She has two sons and two daughters-in-law.* Ask students, *Are you an in-law?* (If yes, ask, *Are you close to your daughter, son, sister, brother, mother, or father-in-law?*)

Background information and culture note: Lulu Winston and Bertha Bean live in Florida. Their children live in other parts of the United States. In the United States and Canada, grandparents often prefer to live in their own homes, apart from their married children. Many senior citizens in the United States live in Florida. The climate is warm. Housing is generally less expensive than elsewhere.

After the class has read and heard the dialogue, ask, *Is Lulu Winston a good mother-in-law?*

GRAMMAR

A Count Nouns: *A/An* (page 31)

Pronunciation note: *A* and *an* are usually pronounced /ə/ and /ən/

It's a boy.

He's an actor.

Practice the pronunciation by reading all the examples in the Grammar Notes.

A.5 (page 33)
Further practice:

★ Ask students to add other roles. For example, an only child, a volunteer worker, a chauffeur for my family, a good basketball player, a basketball fan.

A.6 (page 34)

Further Practice: Add more categories.

• buildings (museums, hospitals, post offices, banks)
• furniture (lamps, tables, chairs, sofas, dressers, bookcases)
• things in the kitchen (ovens, stoves, dishwashers, cabinets, counters)

You can do this exercise as a game. The group that names the most items wins. One group starts, and the others must name a different item. The group that can think of the most correct items for the category wins.

B   Descriptive Adjectives (page 34)

After students have read Grammar Note 2, indicate that the adjective comes before the noun that it describes.

> a tall man   NOT: a man tall

B.4   (page 36)

Further practice: Point to things in your classroom. Ask students to say something about each thing.

> Teacher: *Tell me about this window (door, desk, blackboard, newspaper, dictionary).*

> Student: *It's dirty (clean, new, dusty, interesting, thick).*

Play a name-association game. One student calls out a noun. Another student calls out an adjective that can go with it.

A: a doctor (a teacher, a plumber, a chair)
B: a kind doctor (a friendly teacher, a good plumber, a comfortable chair)

C   Possessive Adjectives (page 38)

Remind students that a noun must follow all possessive adjectives.

D   *This/These* (page 41)

D.1   (page 42)

Culture note: In the United States and Canada, women's pants come in the following sizes: 2, 4, 6, 8, 10, 12, 14, 16, 18 for women (fuller bodies) and 3, 5, 7, 9, 11, 13, 15 for juniors (usually younger or thinner women).

D.5   (page 44)

Further practice: Bring in stamps or currency from different countries. Pass around the stamps and currency. Students ask each other about the different items.

A: What's this?
B: It's a Canadian dollar.

A: What are these?
B: They're stamps from the Netherlands.
C: No, they're not. They're from Switzerland.

E   Prepositions of Place (page 45)

Near is followed by the object. *Next* is always followed by *to* before the object.

> I'm **near** the door.   I'm **next to** the window.

E.4   (page 48)

Further practice: Collect papers in which students have written about their countries. Read their sentences to the class without naming the country. For example: *This country is between Japan and China. It's near Mongolia. What country is it?* The class guesses the country.

OR

Have students write sentences about different states in the United States or Canadian provinces. Let the class guess the place they are describing.

UNIT 3

INTRODUCTION

CAROL AND HER FAMILY (page 52)

PREVIEW THE MATERIAL.

Before listening to or reading the introduction, discuss the illustrations and personalize the material. Tell students to look at the illustrations. Then ask:

> *How many people are there in this family? How many people are there in your family? The people in this family are different from each other. Are the people in your family alike or different?*

Vocabulary practice: Ask your students to use the adjectives in the box to describe people in their families.

After listening to and reading the introduction, personalize the material. Ask the class:

> *What school subjects are you good in? What subjects are you not so good in? Are you good at any sports? Are you a vegetarian? Is Doug similar to teenagers in your country?*

GRAMMAR

A Questions with *Who, What,* and *Where* (page 54)

Culture note: When Lulu says she's seventy-one years old, Bertha says, "You're not. You're seventy-three." Many older women in North America don't like to tell their age. Ask if that is true in other countries. Is it also true for men?

A.1 (page 55)

Further practice: Look at the world map or the map of the United States and Canada. Ask questions with *where* and *what* about the location and the capitals of different places.

> Examples:
> *Where's the Pacific Ocean?*
>
> *What's the capital of Nova Scotia?*

A.4 (page 56)

Further practice: Ask students to look at the expressions in the chart and to tell where they would find the following items: a sink, a TV, a sofa, a computer, a dishwasher, a toaster, a towel, balloons, a conductor, lots of people, a baseball fan, a boss, a table and chairs, a pillow, a blanket.

B Possessive Nouns and Questions with *Whose* (page 61)

Ask students what the difference is between *my friend's dog, my friends' dog, my friend's dogs,* and *my friends' dogs.*

Ask where the apostrophe goes with singular and plural nouns.

Ask for examples of singular and plural possessive nouns.

B.1 (page 62)

Personalization and further practice with possessive nouns: Look around the class and ask questions about other students. If possible, have students ask the questions:

> *Whose initials are __ __? Whose sweater is blue and green? Whose shoes are shiny? Whose bookbag is full? Whose handwriting is neat? Whose hair is very long?*

C Questions with *When* and *What* + Noun: Prepositions of Time (page 65)

Point out that in the United States and Canada we write dates with the month first:
  1/4/94 OR January 4, 1994
  4/1/94 *or* April 1, 1994

C.3 (page 67)
Talk about when different holidays occur in different countries.

D Ordinal Numbers (page 70)

The rules presented here reflect spoken English. Although *The Chicago Manual of Style* states that dates and streets are written as cardinal numbers, students will more likely encounter dates and street numbers in the more common spoken form, as ordinals. You may wish to point out that in written English the cardinal numbers are more often seen.

UNIT 4

INTRODUCTION

IN THE MOOD FOR PIZZA (page 77)

PREVIEW THE DIALOGUE.

Background information: Elenore and Pete are walking along Second Avenue. They're hungry. They're looking for a pizza place. They're in the mood for pizza.

Culture note: Most Americans and English-speaking Canadians eat their big meal at night. (In the United States the evening meal is usually called dinner. In Canada it is called supper. In Canada dinner is a big meal at midday.) For lunch, people have a sandwich, a hamburger, a salad, or a slice of pizza. Pizza places are popular, inexpensive, fast-food restaurants. They are found throughout North America.

Personalize the material: Ask students: *Are there many pizza places in your neighborhood? Are there any restaurants in your neighborhood? What kind? Are they Chinese? Greek? French? Italian? Mexican? Thai? Is pizza your favorite food? What's your favorite food? What are you in the mood for now?*

Further practice: You may wish to have students do the following role play with a partner.

A: I'm in the mood for _____ (pizza, cake, a sandwich). Is there a good _____ (pizza place, bakery, coffee shop) near here?
B: Yes. There's a good _____ on _____ street.
  OR
  No. There aren't any _____ near here.
  OR
  I'm sorry. I don't know.

GRAMMAR

A Imperatives; Suggestions with *Let's* (page 79)

This is the first time you will be introducing verbs other than *be*. Ask students for examples of other verbs besides *walk*. Write the verbs in the base form on the blackboard.

As you read the different uses of the imperative, provide examples and ask students for additional ones.

  Commands: *Stand. Sit. Walk. Don't move. Hands up.*

  Directions: *Turn left. Make a U-turn. Walk down the street. Drive to the next traffic light. Take the Number 4 Bus.*

  Advice or suggestions: *Take it easy. See a doctor. Study this evening. Get a life. Take two pills a day. Come back in a week.*

Requests: *Please show me your notes. Please write soon. Please open the door.*

Warnings: *Be careful. Watch out.*

Punctuation note: For emphasis, use an exclamation mark at the end of a command.

Stop!

A.5 (page 82)

Culture note: Doug is giving directions to a new student in his high school. Schools in the United States and Canada are generally divided as follows:

Nursery School—for children 3 and 4 years old (These are private and optional.)

Kindergarten—for children 4 or 5 years old

Primary School—1st grade through 6th grade (6 to 12 years old) or 1st grade through 8th grade

Junior High School (or Middle School)—7th through 9th grade (or 6th through 8th grade)

High School—10th through 12th grade (or 9th through 12th grade)

A.9 (page 84)

This activity can be done throughout the term. It is especially effective on cold days. Once students get the hang of the game, the leader can speak faster and faster and add different parts of the body (eyebrows, lips, throat, elbow, ankle).

A.11 (page 85)

Find the warnings in the Grammar Notes of the Student Book (*Be careful!*, *Note*, *Remember*).

Ask for warnings for drivers and pedestrians (*Yield, Walk, Don't walk*).

C   There Is/There Are (page 88)

Students may ask if it is wrong to say *a book is on the table* instead of *there's a book on the table*.

Both are grammatically correct. However the second is a more natural statement, and students should use *there is/there are* when pointing out things.

To make sure students can identify the *subject* of sentences, write or dictate these sentences and ask students to underline the subject in each one.

1. There are two books on the shelf.
2. They are new students.
3. Carol's a new student.
4. Carol's initials are C. W.

C.3 (page 90)

Point out that word order is important in English, and incorrect word order sometimes changes the meaning: There's a man in the house.   There's a house in the man.

D   Numbers and Quantifiers (page 93)

D.1 (page 94)

Culture note: Marking systems vary from school to school.

• Percentage grades: 100 percent to 0 percent. Usually the lowest passing grade is 65 percent.

• Letter grades: A, B, C, D, and F. D is the lowest passing grade.

• Numbers: 4, 3, 2, 1. 4 is equal to an A. 1 is the lowest passing grade.

D.2 (page 94)

★ It is difficult to teach basic-level students the distinction between *few* and *a few*. If the question comes up, tell students that *few* indicates a small amount whereas *a few* means *some*.

E Questions with *Is there, Are there,* and *How many* (page 95)

E.4 (page 97)

 Ask students who enjoy puzzles to bring some interesting ones to class.

E.7 (page 99)

 Work in groups. Prepare a quiz with ten questions that begin with *How many.*

F *And/But* (page 99)

F.4 (page 102)

Further practice: Ask students to finish these sentences with *and* and with *but.*

1. She's sick **but she's in class**.
   She's sick **and tired**.
2. He's rich but _____ .
   He's rich and _____ .
3. It's cold but _____ .
   It's cold and _____ .
4. We're hungry but _____ .
   We're hungry and _____ .
5. They're old but _____ .
   They're old and _____ .

UNIT 5

INTRODUCTION

MY POOR BABY IS DOING THE LAUNDRY (page 109)

PREVIEW THE DIALOGUE.

Background and culture note: In this conversation Lulu is calling from Florida. She wants to speak to her son, Pete. She's surprised that Pete's doing the laundry and that Elenore is doing the taxes. She thinks that doing the laundry is a woman's job and doing taxes is a man's job.

Explain that *doing the laundry* usually means putting clothes and detergent in a washing machine, not washing by hand.

Doing taxes usually means filling out forms for the government. Sometimes people go to accountants to do their taxes, but there is still a lot of paperwork that needs to be done in preparation.

In the United States and Canada people pay federal, state, and sometimes local taxes. Taxes from the previous year are due in April in both countries.

After the class has heard the conversation and completed the comprehension check, you may want to ask if anyone knows a woman who is doing a traditional male job or a man who is doing a traditional female job. Offer an example:

> *My girlfriend is a police officer. My uncle is a nurse.*

Ask if there are differences in different countries. For example, many medical doctors in Russia are women, whereas only a few medical doctors in Korea are women.

Optional Role Play: Students work with a partner and practice the conversation. They ask about Pete, Doug, and Elenore, using the words in the box.

Pete	at the laundromat	doing the laundry
Doug	at the supermarket	buying groceries
Elenore	at home	doing the taxes

Example:

A: Where's **Pete**?

B: He's **at the laundromat**.

A: What's he doing?

B: He's **doing the laundry**.

GRAMMAR

A Present Progressive: Affirmative and Negative Statements (page 111)

The present and past progressive are not labeled tenses because linguists today consider the present progressive an aspect of the present tense and the past progressive an aspect of the past tense.

Remind students that there are two negative contractions for all subjects except *I*.

You're not working.   You aren't working.

We're not reading.   We aren't reading.

He's not playing.   He isn't playing.

Remind students that *be* is always a part of the present progressive except when there is one subject and more than one verb.

I'm studying.   He**'s** reading.

NOT: I studying.   He reading.

BUT: He's watching TV and studying.

NOT: He's watching TV and is studying.

A.6 (page 114)

After completing this exercise, you may wish to show students magazine pictures or copies of famous paintings. Then ask students to tell the class about the pictures.

B Present Progressive: *Yes/No* Questions and Short Answers (page 117)

Remind students that *Am*, *Is*, or *Are* begin yes/no questions in the present progressive.

Is he dancing? NOT: He dancing?

B.4 (page 119)

After doing this activity with a partner, do it with the entire class. One student goes to the front of the class and is blindfolded. The class asks the student *yes/no* questions about the class.

C Present Progressive: *Wh-* Questions (page 120)

This is the first time questions with *why* and *who(m)* are introduced.

Since this text introduces students to everyday spoken language, the informal *who* rather than *whom* is often used when asking about an object, and sentences can end with a preposition.

Who are you talking to? NOT: To whom are you talking?

D Present Progressive: Extended Time (page 126)

While the concept of the present progressive for extended time is difficult, the presentation here is simple enough for beginners to learn. To demonstrate the idea of the present progressive for extended time, you can talk about your own teaching schedule.

This year I'm teaching three classes. I'm teaching the basic level, the intermediate level, and the advanced level.

(Right now I'm not teaching the intermediate level or the advanced level.)

D.1 and D.3   (pages 127 and 128)

Culture note: Colleges away from home in the United States and Canada offer students an opportunity to learn about life. Though grades and professional goals are important, many people consider the college experience more than just a time for studying and preparing for a job. It is a time to learn independence, to develop one's interests, and to discover one's goals in life.

Most colleges in the United States today are very expensive. Costs range from about $9,000 a year for a state school to about $25,000 for a private school. Many parents and students take out loans to cover their college expenses. Most college students work during the summer.

UNIT 6

INTRODUCTION

CLOTHES FOR A TEENAGER (page 134)

PREVIEW THE DIALOGUE.

Background: Talk about the title. Make certain students understand that a teenager is a person between the ages of thirteen and nineteen. In this conversation, Elenore is shopping for clothes for Doug. He wants a big college sweatshirt because his friends wear them. His mother isn't certain he needs one. She thinks he needs a dress shirt and dress shoes. Doug wants to dress like his friends. Ask students about teenagers in their country. Do they want to dress alike, too?

> Ask: *What are teenagers wearing these days? Are tight clothes, long skirts, shorts, jeans with holes, or sweatshirts in style today? Are any students wearing T-shirts or sweatshirts with writing on them?*

After students have read and heard the dialogue, talk about the second illustration of Doug. Ask your students:

> *Why is Doug smiling?* (He has a new sweatshirt.) *In your opinion, is it right for a parent to buy a teenager the clothes he wants? Was it right for Elenore to buy Doug the expensive sweatshirt? Why or why not?*

Optional role play: Selling and buying. Tell students to work with a partner and practice the conversation.

Salesperson: Do you need help?

Customer: Yes, I need a **sweatshirt**. (long skirt, T-shirt)

Salesperson: Well, these **sweatshirts** are very popular this year.

Customer: Do you have one in large?

Salesperson: Yes, I do. They come in all sizes.

GRAMMAR

A   Simple Present Tense: Affirmative and Negative Statements (page 136)

You might want to tell students that the "simple present" is neither "simple" nor "present." Show them the meaning of *I play tennis every Monday* on a time line.

PAST ———————————————————— FUTURE

NOW

(Right now it is Tuesday, so I'm not playing tennis.)

Remind students to use an -s or -es with the third person singular.

> He walks to school. She watches TV at night.

Remind students that the negative of the simple present tense always uses the base form after *don't* (*do not*) or *doesn't* (*does not*).

> We don't **speak** Greek.

> It doesn't **rain** there.

A.1 (page 137)

To review material in previous units, ask students which sentences use the present progressive (5, 8) and which one uses the imperative (3).

A.2 (page 137)

Explain syllables. Ask students to look up a few words in the dictionary and to tell you the number of syllables in each word. At this time you may wish to show students how to hyphenate between syllables when a word is broken at the end of a line.

> The baby is **begin-**

ning to talk.

A.5 (page 139)

Ask students about Doug: *Does Doug have an earache? Is he really sick? What's his real problem? Do you know anyone like Doug?*

A.6 (page 139)

You may wish to use this exercise as a model for students to tell or write about themselves and their families.

A.13 (page 144)

★ This exercise has several parts and is more difficult than the earlier exercises. You might want your students to prepare the final part of this exercise (in which they describe an animal) at home and then bring their descriptions to class.

B   Simple Present Tense: *Yes/No* Questions and Short Answers (page 146)

B.8 (page 151)

At the end of this exercise students are asked to criticize the questionnaire. Encourage them to look at all the material in the text with a critical eye.

C   Simple Present Tense: *Wh-* Questions (page 152)

Producing the correct question with *who* may be difficult for students at this stage. Students may only be able to recognize and understand the concept. However, with each new tense they will be given a chance to work with *who* questions again.

C.8 (page 157)

This exercise often leads into a discussion about the roles of men, women, and children in different cultures.

C.10 (page 158)

Trivia-type questions get students to use the grammar form unconsciously while focusing on the content. Interest is usually high, and a great deal of incidental learning takes place. Sometimes students write extremely difficult questions. It's a good idea to check the questions before students ask others.

D   Simple Present Tense and *This/That/These/Those* (page 160)

Some students don't hear the difference between *this* /ð ɪs/ and *these* /ð iʸz/. Test your class's comprehension by having the class call out "number 1" for *this* and "number 2" for *these*.

> Say: *this, these, these, this, this.*

Then ask students to write the number 1 or 2 on a piece of paper after you say *these, these, this, this, these, these* (2,2,1,1,2,2).

E   *One/Ones* (page 164)

First you may wish to show nouns and noun phrases.

noun   noun phrase

I want a **book**   I want **a book about France**.

Then, as you go through the grammar notes, ask students to give another example for each note.

                        singular count noun

1. Do you want   **a hamburger?**

    Yes, I want   **one.**

                   noun phrase

    Do you want **a hamburger with ketchup?**

    Yes, I want   **one.**

2. Where's **the car?**   **It's** in the garage.

    Where's **his car?**   **It's** on Main Street.

    Where's **that car?**   **It's** over there.

    Do you have **a car?**   Yes. **It's** in the garage. (**It** is used in place of **my car,** not **a car.**)

3. We sell gold **earrings** and silver **earrings.** The gold **ones** cost \$30, and the silver **ones** cost \$20.

4. A: Do you have this **stamp?**

    B: No, but I have that **one.**

UNIT 7

INTRODUCTION

ROOMMATE TROUBLE (page 174)

PREVIEW THE DIALOGUE.

Background and culture note: In this conversation Carol and Yoko are arguing because Carol leaves her clothes and papers on Yoko's desk and chair. Yoko would like to keep the apartment neat and clean, while Carol doesn't care if it is messy.

It is not unusual for American college students to pay little attention to housekeeping.

Personalize the material: Ask your students:

> *Do you have a roommate?*
>
> *Is he/she neat and clean? Are you? Do you make your bed every day?*
>
> *Do you like a neat home?*

GRAMMAR

A   Simple Present Tense and Present Progressive: *How often;* Questions of Frequency; Adverbs and Expressions of Frequency (page 176)

Questions that begin with *how often* can be answered with an adverb or an expression of frequency. Sometimes an expression of frequency is better because an adverb of frequency is too vague:

How often does your class go to language laboratory?   Often. (vague)   Twice a week. (better)

Sometimes when we complain, we use the adverb of frequency *always* with the present progressive. The simple present tense is also correct.

They're always fighting.	They always fight.
He's always watching TV.	He always watches TV.

B   Non-Action (Stative) Verbs (page 185)

In some parts of North America, non-action verbs may be used in the present progressive when the action is taking place now. However, it is never wrong to use the simple present tense in those instances.

I'm hearing you.	I hear you.

B.9   (page 192)

A description of the cartoons should elicit the present progressive while a discussion about them should elicit the simple present tense.

C   Verb + Noun or Infinitive: *Like, Prefer, Want, Need* (page 193)

★ You may wish to point out that some verbs are followed by the infinitive while others are followed by the gerund. Other verbs can be followed by either the infinitive or the gerund.

I **need to see** him.	I **enjoy seeing** him.
We **decided to play** golf.	She **avoids playing** golf.
She **likes to travel**.	She **likes traveling**.

C.3   (page 194)

★ To do this exercise correctly, students must recognize the verbs followed by another verb and the verbs followed by an object.

D   Possessive Adjectives and Possessive Pronouns (page 196)

You add an *s* to the possessive adjective for every case except *my*, which becomes *mine*, and *his*, which remains the same because it ends in an *s*.

UNIT 8

INTRODUCTION

THANKSGIVING DAY (page 206)

PREVIEW THE MATERIAL.

Background: Carol is calling her mother the day after Thanksgiving. This was Carol's first Thanksgiving day away from her family. She spent her Thanksgiving vacation visiting San Francisco with her roommate, Yoko.

Culture note: Thanksgiving Day is celebrated in the United States on the fourth Thursday in November. Families and friends gather and share a big meal that usually includes turkey, sweet potatoes (or yams), cranberry sauce, and pumpkin pie.

Personalize the material: Ask students about a similar holiday in their country. Discuss different holidays. Ask students how they celebrated their last holiday.

After students have heard and read the introductory dialogue, ask students, *Has anyone visited San Francisco?* If yes, ask, *When did you go there? How long did you stay? What did you do there?* Then ask, *What's your favorite city? When did you visit it last? How long did you stay there? What did you see?*

Optional role play: Talking about the past.

Have students work with a partner to practice the conversation. Ask them to use the words in the box.

great	invited some friends to my house
wonderful	went to a concert
nice	watched TV
bad	visited a friend
terrible	studied English
awful	cleaned my apartment
	washed my clothes
	had a fight with my friend

A: Did you have a nice weekend?

B: Oh, I had a great weekend. Saturday night I **invited some friends to my house**. Then, on Sunday we **went to a concert**. What about you?

A: I didn't do anything special. I **cleaned my apartment**. Then I **washed my clothes**.

GRAMMAR

A Simple Past Tense: Regular Verbs, Affirmative and Negative Statements (page 208)

Remind students to use the base form with the negative.

Remind students that *did* appears with negative, not affirmative, statements.

 Did appears in affirmative statements only for special emphasis or to contradict a previous statement.

> A: You didn't pay him.
>
> B: You're wrong. I **did** pay him.

A.4 (page 211)

Further practice: Ask students to write a postcard to a friend in a different city. Use this exercise as a model.

B Simple Past Tense: Irregular Verbs, Affirmative and Negative Statements (page 215)

Sometimes it is helpful to give students a five-minute oral quiz on the irregular past-tense form. Each day for several days ask students to study twenty verb forms from the chart on page A17 in Appendix 12. The class stands. After you read the base form, a student must give the correct pronunciation of the past-tense form. If a student makes a mistake, he or she sits down. Develop speed and rhythm. The last student standing wins. Though this is rote memorization, all the verbs will be practiced in context as you go through units 8 and 9.

B.3 (page 218)

Further practice: Ask what your students did on their last school vacation.

B.4 (page 219)

Some students may have heard a different version of this story. Ask them to tell the class the way they heard this story.

B.7 (page 221)

Students may look at the chart of irregular verbs on page A17 as they do this exercise.

B.8 and B.9 (page 222)

These exercises will take more time than the previous ones. You may wish to have students prepare them at home.

C Simple Past Tense: *Yes/No* Questions and Short Answers (page 222)

Did you often sounds like /dɪdʒə/.

C.3 (page 225)

Give your class an oral exercise contrasting *Do, Does, Did.*

> *Do you usually _____? (come on time, eat a big lunch, study at night, watch TV)*
>
> *Did you _____? (come late yesterday, eat a pizza last week, wear jeans to class on Monday, write a letter last night)*
>
> *Does Juan often _____? (ask questions, laugh in class, sit near the door)*

C.4 (page 226)

After students have done this exercise in groups, you may wish to do it as a class. Ask one or two students for questions and have the group ask further questions.

WRAP IT UP (PAGE 233)

Writing suggestion: Before students prepare their compositions, you may wish to go over the reading selections on page 219 and page 228 once again.

UNIT 9

INTRODUCTION

LOVE IS BLIND (page 237)

PREVIEW THE DIALOGUE.

Background note: Pete is talking to his mother. He's upset because he thinks his seventy-three-year-old mother is going out with a ladies' man who is a lot younger than his mother.

Ask students, *What's a ladies' man?* (Some may understand Don Juan or Casanova.)

Explain that when you "go out" with or date someone, you are seeing them as a possible romantic partner.

After students have read and heard the conversation, you may want to talk about older women dating younger men.

Optional role play: Asking where someone was.

Have students work with a partner to practice the conversation. Ask them to use the words in the box.

yesterday	at home	caught a cold
last Monday	at the bank	opened an account
the day before yesterday	at the library	needed books for a report

A: Where were you **yesterday**? You weren't in school.
B: I was **at home**.

A: Why were you **at home?**
B: I **caught a cold**.

GRAMMAR

A Past Tense of *Be*: Affirmative and Negative Statements, *Yes/No* Questions, and Short Answers (page 238)

Point out the differences of form for the past tense of *be* and the past tense of all other verbs.

Affirmative: *Be* has two forms. Other verbs have one form for all persons.

| (be) I **was** late. | (come) I **came** late. |
| We **were** late. | We **came** late. |

Negative:

| (be) It **wasn't** expensive. | (cost) It **didn't cost** much money. |

Yes/No questions:

| (be) **Was** she a student? | (study) **Did** she **study**? |
| **Were** they students? | **Did** they **study**? |

A.4 (page 242)

Talk about sales, final sales, and returning things to a store.

A.5 (page 243)

Ask students questions beginning with *Was, Were, Do, Does, Is,* and *Are.*

Was it **warm** yesterday? (cold, humid, hot, comfortable, windy, cloudy)

Were you **late** today? (early, on time)

Did you **study English** last night? (listen to the news, read the newspaper, do the dishes, talk on the telephone)

Do you usually **eat a big breakfast**? (skip breakfast, wear earrings, drink coffee in the morning, watch TV at night, come to school by bus, walk to school, play ball on weekends, relax in the evening)

Does your family like **spicy food**? (plain food, to travel, to play sports, to go to the movies, to listen to classical music)

Is your watch **slow**? (fast, on time)

Are your shoes **comfortable**? (tight, loose, new, old)

A.8 (page 244)

You may wish to expand this into a written assignment. Ask students to write about what a partner was like as a child.

Example: Bekir was a stubborn child. One day his parents wanted him to clean his room. He refused. They said he couldn't go to his best friend's birthday party if he didn't clean his room. He really wanted to go to the party, but he didn't want to clean his room. He sat in his room and cried all day. He didn't go to the party, and he didn't clean his room.

B Simple Past Tense of *Be*: *Wh-* Questions (page 246)

You may wish to contrast *wh-* questions with *Be* and *wh-* questions with other verbs.

B.1 (page 247)

Some students are interested in American history, and some know a great deal about American history. You may wish to follow up on this lesson and ask students about another country's struggle for independence.

When was it?

Was there a leader? Who was he or she?

Was it a long struggle?

When is Independence Day celebrated in that country?

Practice the expression "to be born."

> *He was born in _____.*   *I was born in _____.*   *Where were you born?*

B.6   (page 252)

If students can't think of their own questions, you may wish to offer these examples to help give them ideas.

1. Who discovered radium? (Madame Curie)
2. Who discovered the theory of relativity? (Einstein)
3. Who painted "The Water Lilies"? (Monet)
4. Who painted "Guernica"? (Picasso. It shows the horrors of war during the Spanish Civil War)
5. Who discovered ways to use electricity? (Thomas Edison)
6. Who invented the telephone? (Alexander Graham Bell)
7. Who were The Beatles (A famous singing group)
8. When did Hawaii become the fiftieth state of the United States? (1959)
9. When was the UN founded? (1945)

C   Simple Past Tense of *Be: There was/There were* (page 253)

Tell students to be careful not to confuse *they were* and *there were*. To help them avoid the confusion, ask students to label the subject and verb in the following sentences.

          Subject   Verb
         They   **were** students.

                 Verb   Subject
         There   **were**   **students and teachers** at the party.

          Subject   Verb
         They   **were** on the bus.

                 Verb   Subject
         There   **were**   **ten people** on the bus.

C.2   (page 255)

Ask students if they had ever lived in a terrible dormitory, hotel, camp, or apartment. Ask if they had had a good time or a bad time. Give an example such as the following:

> My daughter went to a summer camp five years ago. The cabins were ancient. The mattresses were very thin. There wasn't any hot water. There were mosquitoes, ants, and snakes. The living conditions were terrible, but my daughter loved that camp and returned for two more years.

UNIT 10

INTRODUCTION

CAROL AND YOKO HAVE A PARTY (page 265)

PREVIEW THE DIALOGUE.

Background note: In this conversation Carol and Yoko are preparing for a party. Bekir visits and offers to help them. They ask him to go to the supermarket and buy some groceries for the party. When he returns, Carol tells him that he had bought the wrong tuna fish. Instead of regular tuna, he bought tuna for cats.

Personalize the material: Ask students: *What kind of parties do you like? Big ones? Small ones? What kind of food do people usually serve? Do friends bring food to parties? What do your friends usually do at parties? Dance? Sing? Eat? Talk? Listen to music?*

After students have heard and read the conversation, ask them if they ever bought the wrong thing at a store? (There's usually one student who bought or almost bought dog or cat food.)

GRAMMAR

A Count and Non-count Nouns and Quantifiers (page 267)

This is the first presentation of non-count nouns and *some* and *any*, although students have seen and heard examples in previous units. You may wish to turn to the list of common non-count nouns in the Appendix (page A12) and practice using them with *much, many, a few,* or *a little.*

> For example, **I didn't have any coffee this morning.**
>
> **I ate a little bread and cheese for lunch.**

 Some nouns are both count or non-count.

> (cake)   I bought **two cakes** for the party.
>
> Would you like **some cake**?
>
> (chicken) There are **four chickens** in the yard.
>
> I'd like **some chicken** and potatoes.

A.1 (page 268)

As you go over these sentences, you may want to familiarize students with other count and non-count nouns by asking for other nouns in place of the circled ones.

A.4 (page 270)

Personalize the sentences in the exercise:

> *Do you want to buy any furniture?*
>
> If yes, *What do you want to buy*?
>
> *Do you need money? Why?*
>
> *Do you receive a lot of junk mail? Do you get a lot of mail from your family?*

A.8 (page 272)

Ask students what some other countries produce.

A.9 (page 273)

Complaints are a good way to get students talking. You may want to suggest that students discuss good or bad things about their school.

B Count/Non-count Nouns: *Yes/No* Questions; Questions about Quantity: *How much* and *How many* (page 274)

Point out to students that measure words before non-count nouns use *how many* in questions about quantity.

> How much milk do you need?
>
> How many quarts of milk do you need?
>
> How many glasses of milk did he drink?
>
> How many bottles of milk did the baby drink?

B.1 (page 275)

Demonstrate "a pinch" before students listen to this conversation.

After you do this exercise, ask students if they have any good recipes. If yes, ask them to share them with the class. Then you may wish to prepare a short cookbook.

B.6 (page 279)

Personalize the material:

> *How much milk do you use in a week?*
>
> *How much meat would you buy for six people?*
>
> *How much gas does the gas tank in your car hold?*

B.7 (page 279)

Are there any other health questions that you would ask?

B.8 (page 280)

This may lead to discussions about different ways of shopping for things in different places.

C   Enough + Noun, *Too much/Too many/Too little/Too few* + Noun (page 281)

You may wish to point out that adjectives precede *enough* in contrast to nouns which follow.

> adjective + *enough*
>
> He's **old enough** to drive.
>
> *enough* + noun
>
> He has **enough money.**

C.3 (page 283)

In this exercise students have to understand both the grammar and the meaning. In item 1, *There was too little noise* is grammatically correct but doesn't make sense.

D   Modals: *Can* and *Could* for Ability and Possibility; *May I, Can I,* and *Could I* for Polite Requests (page 286)

This is the first formal introduction to the modals. Ask students for examples of different modals.

I can sing.	I have to sing.
You could sing.	I ought to sing.
He should sing.	
We might sing.	
She must sing.	
They will sing.	

Explain that modals have more than one meaning.

> Permission: Can I please see your driver's license?
>
> Ability: She can type.
>
> Possibility: You can take the number 4 train to get to the center of the city.

D.1 (page 288)

You may want to discuss the meaning of the modals in each sentence.

1. She can lift 100 pounds. (ability)
2. She can't smell anything. (lack of ability)

3. I couldn't see the chalkboard. (lack of ability)
4. You couldn't swim. (lack of possibility)
5. We could see the ocean and the beach. (possibility)
6. They can't hear us. (lack of possibility)
7. He can't understand you. (lack of ability)

UNIT 11

INTRODUCTION

WHAT DID YOU SAY? (page 303)

PREVIEW THE DIALOGUE.

Background note: In this conversation Bertha tells Lulu she's going to the ear, nose, and throat doctor to get a hearing aid. Lulu, whose hearing is not so good, at first doesn't want to admit that she too may need a hearing aid. Many older people become hard of hearing. Discuss other problems that older people face.

After students have heard and read the dialogue, ask students to describe Lulu's personality. Is she vain? Is she funny? Is she strong-willed?

GRAMMAR

A *Be Going to* for the Future (page 305)

True beginners should be aware of the three forms of the future, but should not have to worry about deciding which is appropriate. The most appropriate form will be more easily discernible for students at a higher level.

Go over the time markers and ask for examples.

A.6 (page 312)

Further practice: To contrast the past and future, ask students the following:

> *When are you going to (take a trip, finish this course, watch TV, go to the movies, buy a new car, go to the post office)?*

> *When did you (buy your watch, speak to your best friend, read the paper, watch TV, go to the bank, write a letter)?*

A.9 (page 314)

This memory game will assure you that students know the form and are pronouncing it correctly. Sometimes when students use "gonna," they make the mistake of saying "gonna to."

A.10 (page 314)

This can become a written assignment. Students can use one of the pictures as a guide and write a story.

B Present Progressive for the Future (page 315)

Students tend to avoid using the present progressive for the future. However, native speakers use it very often, particularly with the verb *go*.

C *Will* for the Future (page 320)

As you go through the Grammar Notes, ask for more examples.

Ask students for other predictions. (*Will people use picture telephones? Will more students have lap-top computers? Will people get taller? As women work at traditional male jobs, will they die younger?*)

Ask students to pretend to sell things they have to their classmates.

Student A: My purse is on sale for $25.00.

Student B: I'll buy it.

Student A: I'm selling my shoes for $20.00.

Student B: I'll buy them.

Point out that there is only one negative contraction for *will*, that is, *won't*.

D   Modals: *May* or *Might* for Possibility (page 328)

If students ask about the word *maybe*, explain that *maybe* is an adverb and it usually comes at the beginning of a sentence.

> Maybe he will work for his father. = He may work for his father.

UNIT 12

INTRODUCTION

YOU CAN WIN MORE BEARS WITH HONEY (page 338)

PREVIEW THE MATERIAL.

Background note: One evening at dinner Elenore complains to Pete that his new secretary forgot to give Pete the message that Elenore had called. In addition, the new secretary wasn't as friendly or polite as Pete's former secretary.

The next evening Elenore tells Pete that his new secretary had been friendlier, more efficient, and more confident on the phone. Elenore asks if he had complained to her. Pete says that he hadn't criticized her. He found something nice to say to her. Elenore remarks that he was smart and recalls the expression, "You can win more bears with honey."

You may wish to talk about secretaries. Ask students what a good secretary needs to do (type well, answer politely, be friendly, work accurately, etc.).

You may wish to talk about getting a job. Talk about writing resumes, having an interview, giving references for a job.

After students have read and heard the conversation, discuss the saying "You Can Win More Bears with Honey" with your class. Ask if anyone remembers a situation in which he or she accomplished more by being nice rather than critical.

Talk about why the secretary was bad the first day. (She was nervous, she was busy at that time.)

GRAMMAR

A   Comparative Form of Adjectives (page 340)

You may wish to have two students (A and B) stand in front of the class and demonstrate the rules for the comparative form of adjectives given in the Grammar Notes.

> Grammar Note 2
> (young) A is young**er than** B.
> (large) A's dictionary is larg**er than** B's.
>
> Grammer Note 3
> (expensive) A's pen is **more** expensive **than** B's.
> (busy) A's busi**er than** B.
>
> Grammar Note 4
> (tired) A went to bed at 1:00 A.M. B went to bed at 11:00 P.M.
> They both got up at seven o'clock. A is **more** tired **than** B.
> (quiet) B is usually quiet**er than** A.

Grammar Note 5

A's pen is **less** expensive **than** B's.

Grammar Note 6

B's pen is **better than** A's.

A.5 (page 345)

Go over these expressions with the class. Ask your students if they can think of instances from their lives in which these expressions seemed appropriate.

A.6 (page 346)

Students can write the questions at home and bring them in the next day. If your class has students from different countries, many interesting conversations can take place comparing the country you are all in now and the countries students have come from.

A.7 (page 346)

After students have completed the exercise with a partner, ask them to use the adjectives and tell about people they know.

> Example: My uncle is much more generous than my aunt.

> My uncle always gives his children, his nieces, and nephews expensive gifts. My aunt always says he's foolish. She says they need to save for their future.

B   Adverbs of Manner; Comparative Form of Adverbs (page 347)

Adverbs of manner usually answer the question **how?**

> Example: She types quickly.

> **A:** How does she type?

> **B:** Quickly.

B.6 (page 352)

Expansion: Have students say a sentence with a meaning that is different from the words.

> Example: I love you. (Say it questioningly. Say it sadly. Say it angrily.)

B.8 (page 353)

First check the form. Then discuss the ideas behind the questions.

C   Adjective + *Enough; Too* + Adjective; *Very* + Adjective (page 354)

You may wish to contrast the position of *enough* with adjectives and the position of *enough* with nouns. Tell students to complete the sentences with *enough* + the word in parentheses.

1. There weren't _____ . (people)

2. He's not _____ . (tall)

3. She didn't have _____ . (time)

4. We aren't _____ . (old)

C.7 (page 358)

Ask students to bring in a birthday card. Compare the different cards.

D   *As* + Adjective/Adverb + *As; The same* + Noun + *As; The same as; Different from* (page 360)

Tell students that *as . . . as* is used more often in the negative or in a question than in the affirmative.

Students often make the mistake of putting an adjective rather than a noun after *the same* + noun + *as*. (*He is the same tall as my brother.*)

E *More/Less/Fewer* + Noun; Comparative Form of Adjective + Noun (page 366)

This is a good time to review the count and non-count nouns.

WRAP IT UP (PAGE 370)

As an additional exercise, bring in brochures from department stores. Give them to small groups of students and ask them to discuss what they see.

> Example:
>
> A: These are great beach towels. They look very soft and fluffy.
>
> B: But they're very expensive. They're $45.00 a towel.
>
> C: How about these towels? They're much less expensive.
>
> D: But they're much smaller.

UNIT 13

INTRODUCTION

SURPRISE VISITORS (page 375)

PREVIEW THE DIALOGUE.

Elenore and Pete went to a party on the wrong night. They were very embarrassed because their hosts were unprepared for visitors. Ask students, *Have you ever made this kind of mistake? What happened?*

GRAMMAR

A Past Progressive: Affirmative and Negative Statements, *Yes/No* Questions and Answers, *Wh*-Questions (page 377)

The form of the past progressive is the same as the present progressive except that *be* is in the past.

It may take a while before all your students understand the difference between the questions

> *What did you do when your teacher came in?*
>
> AND
>
> *What were you doing when your teacher came in?*

A.1 (page 379)

There are different possible answers, and you may wish to discuss them with your students. One answer is best, but the others are also possible. Ask students to explain their answers.

For example: *We were driving to work when he called me on the telephone.* (A student may explain that he or she has a car telephone.)

A.5 (page 381)

Students can first work alone and then check their answers with a partner. This way they will have more chances of correcting themselves before they listen to it on a cassette.

A.6 (page 383)

This type of exercise gives you the chance to see if students know the form.

A.8 (page 383)

Everyone has experienced special events, but often it is difficult to remember them in class. Go over the examples and add one or two from your life to help students recall events from their lives.

A.9 (page 384)

You may wish to have students prepare this at home.

B Direct and Indirect Objects (page 385)

You can use *for* after some of the verbs listed in the category with *to*. In this case *for* means *instead of*. (*Would you read that story for me? I don't have time to read it.*)

However, this is not an example of direct and indirect objects.

B.4 (page 389)

Ask students if they know anyone who is like Jack or Ron.

B.7 (page 391)

This exercise has a new form. Students must listen for the differences between the written text and the audio cassette.

B.11 (page 393)

You may wish to expand this into a discussion about gift-giving in different countries. Ask students: *On what occasions do you exchange gifts? Is it common to open a gift immediately or later? Is it less common to write letters nowadays than it was in the past? What about homemade gifts? Are they common? Do you like them?*

B.12 (page 394)

You may want to ask students to write a few words on the blackboard in their language and then explain, pronounce, and translate them for the class.

C *Too/Either* (page 395)

When practicing *too* and *either* you can review all the tenses and modals studied so far.

It is confusing to practice *so* and *neither* at the same time as you do *too* and *either*. If students ask about this form, don't practice it until after they have done the exercises with *too* and *either*.

D Phrasal Verbs with Direct Objects (page 401)

This is one of the most difficult items for students to learn and remember since there is often no logic behind one or another particle, and yet the particle can completely change the meaning of an entire sentence.

> I put on my hat.

> I put away my hat.

E Phrasal Verbs without Objects (page 408)

Some of these phrasal verbs have another meaning that can take a direct object.

> Hang your coat up.

> He cleared the problem up for us.

> They broke it down into its elements.

UNIT 14

INTRODUCTION

CAROL'S NEWS (page 417)

PREVIEW THE DIALOGUE.

Background note: Carol calls her parents and starts to give them some very important news. She tells them that she is engaged to a handsome poet. Before she can explain further, they get cut off. Elenore and Pete are alarmed, but when they try to call her back, the line is busy. Students are left wondering what is going on until the Wrap It Up section. There they get more details about her boyfriend and about what Carol's parents would be.

Ask students: *Where do people often meet their future husbands and wives? Do parents introduce young people to each other? Do they go on blind dates? Do young people meet at school? Do people meet at work? Do you think Pete and Elenore are happy to hear that Dan's a poet? Why or why not?*

Carol's twenty years old. Ask students: *Is that a young age to get married? At what age do people usually marry and start a family in a country you know well? Are people marrying earlier or later?*

GRAMMAR

This unit presents modals and the superlative form of adjectives and adverbs. The modals have been spread out over three units, and the superlative form has been separated from the comparative form so that students will not be presented with too many similar structures at the same time.

A *Should* (page 419)

A.5 (page 422)

After students have worked in groups, ask if anyone has had any problems similar to the ones they have just read about.

A.6 (page 423)

Ask students to bring in popular expressions in their language. Check them. Then ask the students to write one on the blackboard. Discuss them as a class.

A.8 (page 424)

Encourage students to give ideas about health that they've gotten from their grandmother, their doctor, or their own experience. Compare that advice.

B *Had Better* (page 425)

The contraction of a subject pronoun + *had* is written and pronounced the same as the contraction of the subject pronoun + *would*.

> **I'd** better pay that bill today. (**I had** better pay that bill today.)

> **I'd** like to forget about it. (**I would** like to forget about it.)

C *Have to, Don't have to, Must* (page 429)

Have to is the only modal with two forms: *have to* and *has to*.

Have to and *must* can mean the same thing, but the negative of *have to* and the negative of *must* have different meanings.

> I **don't have to** wear a skirt to school.

> They **mustn't** wear jeans to work.

C.8 (page 435)

Further practice: Ask students, *Was anyone in the army?* If yes, *What did you have to do?*

C.9 (page 436)

By discussing the best way to learn a language, students take responsiblity for their work. This exercise usually provokes a lot of discussion in a language class and allows students to vent any frustrations they may have.

D **Superlative Form of Adjectives and Adverbs** (page 436)

You may wish to begin with a dictation from the fairy tale of "Snow White." Ask students to write the vain stepmother's words, "Mirror, mirror on the wall/ Who's the fairest of them all?"

When going over Grammar Note 6, ask students for other prepositional phrases. (For example, *of the century, in my family, of all, of the year*). Write them on the chalkboard. Ask students to complete the sentences with the superlative form of adjectives or adverbs.

Examples:

It was the worst storm of the century.

She works the hardest in my family.

This was the best cake of all.

Today was the hottest day of the year.

Students often forget to write a plural noun after the superlative with *one of the*. Write these sentences on the chalkboard and ask students to add the noun in parentheses. This is also a way to review the plural form of nouns.

(day) It was one of the coldest _____ of the year.

(man) He is one of the strongest _____ on our team.

(chef) She was one of the best _____ in the world.

(leave) That is one of the most beautiful _____ of your collection.

PUTTING IT ALL TOGETHER

This unit reviews the major grammar structures of the book. There are three parts with both controlled and open-ended exercises. Part A reviews Verb Tenses and Modals. Part B goes over Verb Tenses and Comparisons. Part C covers Verb Tenses and Nouns and Quantifiers.

Tapescript

James Belmont is a photography teacher. Lulu is a new student. Listen and read their conversation.

James Belmont: Hi, I'm James Belmont. What's your name?

Lucille Winston: Lucille Winston.

James: How do you spell Winston?

Lucille: W-I-N-S-T-O-N.

James: What's your first name again?

Lucille: Lucille.

James: How do you spell it?

Lucille: L-U-C-I-L-L-E. My name's Lucille, but everyone calls me Lulu.

James: Lulu?

Lulu: Yes, Lulu.

James: Okay, Lulu. Welcome! Where are you from, Lulu?

Lulu: I'm from Vancouver.

James: Vancouver? Where is Vancouver?

Lulu: It's in Canada. It's here.

The Alphabet (Student Book, page 3)

Listen and repeat the letters of the alphabet.
Aa Bb Cc Dd Ee Ff Gg Hh Ii Jj Kk Ll Mm Nn Oo Pp Qq Rr Ss Tt Uu Vv Ww Xx Yy Zz

UNIT 1:

INTRODUCTION (STUDENT BOOK, PAGE 4)

Pete Winston is in New York, and Milt Singer is in Oregon. Listen and read their telephone conversation.

Milt Singer: Hello.

Pete Winston: Hi, Milt?

Milt Singer: Yes.

Pete Winston: This is Pete Winston.

Milt Singer: Hi, Pete. How are you? How's business?

Pete Winston: I'm fine, and business is great. But I'm worried.

Milt Singer: Why? What's wrong?

Pete Winston: I'm worried about my daughter, Carol.

Milt Singer: Why?

Pete Winston: She's in Oregon, at Oregon State University.

Milt Singer: That's wonderful!

Pete Winston: Yes, it is. But I think she's in love.

Milt Singer: That's wonderful too!

Pete Winston: No, it isn't. I don't know her boyfriend.

Milt Singer: Is he a student?

Pete Winston: No, he isn't.

Milt Singer: Is he a teacher?

Pete Winston: No, he isn't.

Milt Singer: What's his name?

Pete Winston: Rocky.

Milt Singer: Rocky?

Pete Winston: Yes, Rocky! Who is this Rocky? Milt, you're an old friend. You're in Oregon now. You're a great detective. Please help me.

Milt Singer: I'll do my best.

Pete Winston: Thanks, Milt. Bye.

Milt Singer: Bye.

Exercise A.1 (Student Book, page 7) Affirmative Statements

Listen and read the story.

Milt Singer is from Washington, D.C. He is in Oregon now. He is at Oregon State University. He is a detective.

Carol Winston is from New York. Yoko Mori is from Japan. They are roommates. They are new students at Oregon State University.

Oregon State University is big. It is clean and beautiful. The people are friendly. It is a nice place. Carol and Yoko are with Milt. They are with their dog, too.

Exercise B.1 (Student Book, page 9)

*Listen and read this letter from Milt to his sister. Listen again and complete the sentences. Use **I'm, He's,** or **She's**.*

September 8

Hi Janet, I'm in Oregon. I'm working for Pete Winston from New York. He's an old friend. He's a nice man and he's a great businessman. He's worried about his daughter, Carol. She's a new student at Oregon State University. She's in love. Rocky is her boyfriend. He's not a student. Pete is not happy. I want to help him.

Write soon. Give my love to the family.

Love,

Milt

Exercise C.1 (Student Book, page 11)

Listen and read Milt's thoughts.

My work is not easy. Where is Rocky? Who is Rocky? He's not on campus. He's not in the telephone book. He's not with Carol. He's not a student. He's not a teacher. Carol's happy, but Pete's not happy. Pete's worried. But I'm not worried. After all, I'm Milt, the great detective.

Exercise D.1 (Student Book, page 16)

Yoko and Al Brown are outside an ESL class. It is the first day of school. Listen and read their conversation. Then match the questions and answers.

Yoko: Hi. Are you new here?

Al Brown: Yes, I am.

Yoko: I am, too. What's your name?

Al Brown: Al Brown. What's yours?

Yoko: Yoko Mori. Are you a new student?

Al Brown: No, I'm not. Where are you from?

Yoko: I'm from Japan. Where are you from?

Al Brown: I'm from Michigan.

Yoko: Michigan? Then you're not a student in this English class.

Al Brown: You're right. I'm not a new student. I'm a new teacher. I'm your new teacher.

Exercise E.3 (Student Book, page 21)

Listen and complete the sentences.

Milt: Look, over there! Carol and Yoko are with a man. He's saying good-bye. Now, watch me. Remember, I'm Milt, the great detective!
Excuse me, what time is it?

Al: It's one-fifteen.

Milt: Oh, that's good. I'm not late. It's a nice day.

Al: Yes, it is.

Milt: Are you a student?

Al: No, I'm not.

Milt: Ah ha! You're not a student. Is your name Rocky?

Al: No, sorry. It's Al Brown. *(He walks away.)*

Milt: My work is not easy.

WRAP IT UP (STUDENT BOOK, PAGE 24)

Milt and Pete are talking on the telephone. Listen and read their conversation.

Milt: Hello.

Pete: Hi. Is that you, Milt?

Milt: Yes, it is.

Pete: This is Pete. Any news about Rocky?

Milt: No, I'm sorry.

Pete: Carol says, "Rocky is big. He's strong. With Rocky here, I'm safe. I love him."

Milt: I see.

Pete: I ask, "Is Rocky there now?" Carol laughs and says, "Yes, he's always here." Milt, I'm worried.

Milt: Let me think. She says, "He's big and strong." She's safe with Rocky. He's always there. Wait a second. I've got it!

Pete: You do?

Milt: Yes. Rocky is big and strong. He lives with Carol and Yoko.

Pete: What?

Milt: Relax, Pete. Rocky is a dog. Rocky is Yoko's dog.

Pete: Rocky's a dog! Oh, Milt. You're a great detective! And I'm an old, worried father. Please, Milt, don't tell Carol. This is our secret.

UNIT 2:

INTRODUCTION (STUDENT BOOK, PAGE 29)

Lulu Winston and Bertha Bean are friends. Lulu has new pictures of her family. Listen and read the conversation.

Lulu: Come, look at my new pictures.

Bertha: Not more pictures!

Lulu: These are *new* pictures.

Bertha: Okay, Lulu. Show me your pictures.

Lulu: These are my sons. Bob is big and strong. He's a plumber. He's so handsome. His eyes are big and brown. His hair is dark and wavy. Pete is next to him. Pete's a businessman. He's very intelligent.

Bertha: Who's this?

Lulu: It's my brother, Joe.

Bertha: Are these your grandchildren?

Lulu: Yes. They're my wonderful grandchildren. They're very good to me.

Bertha: Who are the women behind your grandchildren?

Lulu: They're my daughters-in-law. My sons are so handsome!

Bertha: They're pretty.

Lulu: Pretty? My sons aren't pretty. They're handsome.

Bertha: Your daughters-in-law are pretty.

Lulu: My daughters-in-law are *lucky*! They're married to my wonderful sons.

Bertha: They're not so lucky. *You're* their mother-in-law!

Exercise A.2 (Student Book, page 32)

*Listen and complete the sentences. Use **a** or **an** before a singular noun. Leave a blank before a plural noun.*

1. He's a plumber.
2. We are students.
3. I'm an engineer.
4. It's a house.
5. This is an apple.
6. These are watches.
7. They're knives.
8. It's an hour.
9. They are businessmen.
10. It's an ice cream cone.

(continued on next page)

11. This is a dictionary.
12. We're teachers.
13. These are earrings.
14. She's an actress.
15. This is an orange.
16. She's a grandmother.
17. This is a hospital.

Exercise B.1 (Student Book, page 35)

Listen to this letter from Carol to Lulu Winston. Then read the letter and find these adjectives. Circle them in the letter.

October 12.

Dear Grandma Lulu,

Thanks so much for the cookies. They're delicious. I'm happy here at Oregon State. My roommate, Yoko, is from Japan. She's a new student, too. She's very nice. She's tall and thin. Her hair is long and straight.

We have a small apartment and a big dog. Our dog's name is Rocky. He's big and loud. We're safe with Rocky around.

My classes are interesting, and my teachers are friendly. I'm lucky to be here.

I hope you're fine. Please write.

Love, Carol

Exercise C.1 (Student Book, page 39)

Carol is showing Yoko a picture of her grandmother. Listen and read their conversation.

Carol: This is my grandmother. Her name is Lulu. She is seventy-three years old. She has two sons. Their names are Peter and Bob. Peter is my father. His nickname is Pete. My mother's name is Elenore.

Yoko: Are your mother and grandmother close?

Carol: No. My mother is not close to my grandmother. My grandmother is old-fashioned. She is a good cook, and her home is very clean. My mother isn't a good cook. Our house is always messy. My grandmother thinks my mother isn't a good wife. My mother thinks my grandmother is a terrible mother-in-law. I love my mother and my grandmother, but when they're together, they fight all the time.

Exercise D.1 (Student Book, page 42)

Lulu is at a new laundromat. She has a problem. Listen and read the conversation between Lulu and the woman who works at the laundromat.

Woman: Is something wrong?

Lulu: Yes.

Woman: What's the problem?

Lulu: Well, this isn't my blouse, and these aren't my socks.

Woman: I'm so sorry.

Lulu: And this isn't my towel. This towel is yellow. My towels are blue. Two of my towels aren't here, and my brown blouse isn't here.

Woman: Oh, no.

Lulu: And look at these jeans. They're a size 8! Look at me. Am I a size 8? I'm a size 18.

Woman: I'm terribly sorry.

Lulu: I am, too.

Exercise E.3 (Student Book, page 47)

Listen to the conversation. Yoko and Carol are very unhappy. There's a cock-roach in their kitchen. Put a check where the cockroach was. Then complete the sentence.

Yoko: Carol, look! Over there, behind you.

Carol: What is it?

Yoko: It's a cockroach.

Carol: Where?

Yoko: On the refrigerator near you.

Carol: Where?

Yoko: Now it's on the counter next to the refrigerator. Here's a shoe.

Carol: *(Bang)*
(Carol bangs shoe to kill roach)

Yoko: Is it dead?

Carol: No, it's under the napkin on the counter. *(Bang)*

Yoko: Now it's between the sink and the stove.

Carol: *(Bang)* It's dead.

Yoko: Thank goodness. I hate roaches.

Carol: Me, too.

Yoko: Oh, no!

Carol: What is it?

Yoko: Another cockroach.

UNIT 3:

INTRODUCTION (STUDENT BOOK, PAGE 52)

Listen and read about Carol and her family. Write the names of the people under their pictures.

Carol Winston is twenty years old. She's a student at Oregon State University. She's pretty, friendly, and funny. She's a little lazy and a little messy. She's good in art, but she isn't good in languages.

Norma is Carol's older sister. She's twenty-four years old. She is divorced and lives in Boston. She's a Spanish teacher. She's good in languages. She loves animals. She's a vegetarian. She's different from Carol. She's serious. They aren't good friends. Their mother, Elenore, is sorry about that.

Doug is Carol's younger brother. He's in high school. He's fifteen years old. He's a good soccer player and he's on his school's team. He's a little lazy about schoolwork. He's hotheaded. He often gets angry. These days Doug and his father disagree a lot. Doug is always on the phone. Doug's radio is always loud. His clothes are very modern and his hairstyle is always strange.

Pete Winston is Norma, Carol, and Doug's father. He is fifty years old. He lives in New York City with his wife and his son. He's a businessman. He is serious. His children think his ideas are old-fashioned. His mother and two daughters live far away, and he often worries about them.

Elenore Lopez Winston is Pete's wife. She is Norma, Carol, and Doug's mother. She is forty-nine years old. She's a writer. She's a terrible cook, and her home is always messy. She likes people and has a lot of friends. She's intelligent and friendly. She gets along well with everyone except her mother-in-law, Lulu Winston.

Lulu Winston is Pete's mother. She is seventy-three years old. She lives in Florida. She lives alone and is often lonely. She's proud of her home. Her apartment is very clean, and she's a wonderful cook. She has two sons and she is very proud of her sons.

Exercise A.3 (Student Book, page 56)

Listen to the conversation between Lulu and Bertha. Write the correct questions.

Lulu: Who's there?

Bertha: It's me, Bertha.

Lulu: Oh, come on in. What's that?

Bertha: It's a small gift.

Lulu: Who's it for?

Bertha: For you. It's October 15th. Happy birthday!

Lulu: Oh, Bertha. Thanks so much. It's heavy. What is it? Is it a book?

Bertha: No, it's a photo album.

Lulu: Thank you, thank you, thank you. I feel like I'm twenty-one, not seventy-one.

Bertha: You're not seventy-one. You're seventy-three.

Lulu: Sh! It's a secret.

Exercise A.4 (Student Book, page 56)

Read the phrases in the box. Listen to the conversation. Then practice the role play that follows.

Jeff's mother: Hello.

Doug Winston: This is Doug. Is Jeff there?

Jeff's mother: Oh, hi, Doug. No, I'm sorry. Jeff isn't here.

Doug: Where is he?

Jeff's mother: He's at a party.

Doug: Please tell him I called.

Noah's father: Hello.

Doug: Hi. This is Doug. Is Noah there?

Noah's father: No, I'm sorry. Noah isn't at home.

Doug: Where is he?

Noah's father: He's at the movies.

Doug: Please tell him I called.

Dino's sister: Hello.

Doug: Hello. This is Doug. Is Dino there?

Dino's sister: Oh, hi, Doug. Dino isn't here now.

Doug: Where is he?

Dino's sister: He's at a ball game.

Doug: Well, please tell him I called.

Mrs. Winston: What's the matter, Doug?

Doug: Jeff is at a party, Noah is at the movies, and Dino is at a ball game. Today is my birthday, and my friends are busy.

Noah, Jeff, Dino: Surprise! Happy birthday! Gotcha!

Doug: You guys are something.

Exercise B.4 (Student Book, page 63)

Al Brown is Yoko's English teacher. He has three papers without names. Listen to the conversation. Then listen again and complete the conversation.

Al Brown: Whose composition is this?

Bekir: Is it a good composition?

Al Brown: It's excellent.

Bekir: It's my composition.

Yolanda: No, that's not your handwriting. It's Yoko's composition. She's absent today.

Al Brown: Thanks, Yolanda. Whose test is this?

Bekir: Is it a good test?

Al Brown: It's okay.

Bekir: I think it's my test.

Juan: It's not your test. It's my test. See, my name is on the back.

Al Brown: Okay, Juan. Here's your test. Whose composition is this?

Bekir: Is it a good composition?

Al Brown: Well, it needs work.

Bekir: It isn't my composition.

Al Brown: Yes, it is. I have a grade for everyone else.

Bekir: Oh.

Exercise C.4 (Student Book, page 67)

There's a meeting every few weeks in Carol and Yoko's building. Listen to the conversation between Yoko and Carol. Then read the questions and circle the correct answers.

Carol: Is the next meeting in November?

Yoko: No, it's in October.

Carol: Is it on Monday, October 29th?

Yoko: No, it's on Tuesday, October 30th.

Carol: Is it in the afternoon?

Yoko: No, it's in the evening.

Carol: Is it at six o'clock?

Yoko: No, it's at six-thirty.

Carol: Is it at our neighbor's apartment?

Yoko: No, it's here.

Exercise D.1 (Student Book, page 70)

Pete and Elenore are going to a party. They are confused. Listen to their conversation. Then listen again and complete the sentences.

Pete: Their apartment is on 72nd Street.

Elenore: No, it's not. Their apartment's on 75th Street.

Pete: It's between First and Second Avenue.

Elenore: No, it's not. It's between Second and Third Avenue.

Pete: It's on the fifth floor.

Elenore: No, it's on the third floor.

Pete: Whose apartment are you talking about?

Elenore: John and Alice's apartment.

Pete: The party isn't at John and Alice's apartment. It's at John and Sue's apartment.

Exercise D.3 (Student Book, page 71)

Listen to the dialogue. Then answer the question below.

Doug: What's the next school holiday?

Noah: Election Day.

Doug: When is it?

Noah: It's on the first Tuesday in November.

Dino: Not always.

Noah: Yes, it is.

Dino: No, it's not. Election Day is on the first Tuesday after the first Monday in November.

Noah: Okay, okay. You're such a genius.

UNIT 4:

INTRODUCTION (STUDENT BOOK, PAGE 77)

Elenore and Pete are walking along Second Avenue in New York City. Listen and read their conversation.

Elenore: It's a beautiful day.

Pete: Yes, it's sunny and clear. There isn't a cloud in the sky.

Elenore: I'm hungry. I'm in the mood for pizza. Let's have pizza for lunch.

Pete: Okay. Is there a pizza place near here?

Elenore: I don't know. There's a young man near you. Ask him.

Pete: Excuse me. Is there a good pizza place near here?

Man: I don't know. There's a Chinese restaurant on this street, and there are two small restaurants on the next street. There are a few coffee shops on 43rd Street, but I don't know of any pizza places near here.

Pete: Thanks anyway. There's a woman over there. Ask her.

Elenore: Excuse me. Is there a pizza place near here?

Woman: Well, there aren't any pizza places near here, but there's a great little pizza place on 37th Street and Third Avenue. Walk straight down Third Avenue to 37th Street. Turn right on 37th Street.

Pete: Okay. Thanks a lot.

Elenore: What street are we on?

Pete: Thirty-seventh Street. Look! There's the pizza place.

Elenore: Finally! I'm really hungry, and I'm tired, too.

Pete: Oh, no!

Elenore: What's wrong?

Pete: There's a sign on the door: "Closed today."

Elenore: Are you really in the mood for pizza?

Pete: Nah.

Exercise A.1 (Student Book, page 80)

There are two burglars in Pete and Elenore's house. Listen and read their conversation.

Frank: Hey, George. I'm nervous. This is my first job.

George: Relax, Frank. I'm here.

Frank: Okay, George. What's this? Is this a gold watch?

George: Yes, it's gold. Take it.

Frank: How about these pearls next to the watch?

George: They're good pearls. Put them in our bag.

Frank: What's that, over there?

George: Junk. Don't take it.

Frank: What's under the junk?

George: It's a ring, but leave it. It's a cheap ring.

Frank: Are these good earrings?

George: Yes, give them to me. (police siren)

Frank: What's that noise?

George: A police siren. Drop everything. Run!

Exercise A.5 (Student Book, page 82)

Doug is at school. There is a new student in his history class. Doug is giving the new student directions. Listen and label each place on the map.

New student: Excuse me. How do I get to the library?

Doug: To get to the library, walk down the hall to the stairs. Go up the stairs to the fourth floor. Turn left.

Student: How do I get to the gym?

Doug: Walk down the hall to the stairs. Go down to the basement. Then turn left.

Student: What about the men's room?

Doug: The men's room is on this floor. Walk down the hall. It's on the left just before the staircase.

Student: How do I get to the computer room?

Doug: Walk down the hall to the stairs. Go down to the second floor. Don't turn left. That's the principal's office. Stay away from him. Turn right. The computer room is the first room on your right.

Student: Thanks a lot.

Doug: No problem. See you around.

Exercise C.4 (Student Book, page 90)

*Listen and complete the sentences. Use **They're (They are)** or **There are**.*

There are two women over there. They are police officers. They're near my car. Oh, no! There are two tickets on my car. Wait! They aren't tickets. They're advertisements. They're advertisements for a new garage and a new car wash.

Now there are two men near my car. They are angry. They're angry at the police officers. There are parking tickets on their cars. Their cars are in a "No Parking" area.

Exercise D.1 (Student Book, page 94)

Al Brown is talking to his students. Listen and match the names with the grades.

Al Brown: Here, Yoko, here's your test.

Yolanda: Wow Yoko! Only one mistake. That's great!

Al Brown: There's no name on this test. Is it your test, Bekir?

Bekir: Yes. Not bad. There are only a few mistakes. Whose test is that? There aren't any mistakes on it.

Al Brown: It's Yolanda's. Here, Yolanda. Congratulations.

Yolanda: Thanks, Mr. Brown.

Al Brown: Here's your test, Mishiko.

Mishiko: Oh, no. There are a lot of mistakes.

Al Brown: I know, but don't worry. This is the first of many tests.

Exercise E.3 (Student Book, page 97)

*Lulu and Bertha are at a restaurant. Listen and read their conversation. Then answer the questions. Check **yes** or **no**.*

Lulu: Look at that delicious cake.

Bertha: Don't eat it.

Lulu: What?

Bertha: Don't eat the cake. It's fattening. There are 300 calories in one piece.

Lulu: How many calories are there?

Bertha: Three hundred. I have a calorie chart here.

Lulu: Who cares?

Exercise F.1 (Student Book, page 100)

*Elenore and Pete Winston are talking about different apartments. Listen and complete the conversation. Use **and** or **but**.*

Elenore: It's difficult to find a good apartment in this city. Joe's apartment is cheap, but it's far from stores. Our apartment is near stores, but it's expensive.

Pete: You're right. My uncle's apartment is cheap, but it's small. Dino's apartment is big and cheap, but it's very dark.

Elenore: Carol and Yoko are lucky. Their apartment is cheap and comfortable. It's near stores, and it's sunny, too.

Pete: But it's in a small college town. It's not in a big city.

UNIT 5:

INTRODUCTION (STUDENT BOOK, PAGE 109)

Elenore is talking to her mother-in-law, Lulu. Listen and read their telephone conversation.

Elenore: Hello.

Lulu: Hi, Elenore. This is Lulu.

Elenore: Hello Lulu. How are you doing?

Lulu: I'm fine. How are my wonderful grandchildren? What are they doing?

Elenore: Everyone's okay. You know, Norma's in Boston. Doug's the captain of his soccer team this year. He's very proud of that. Carol's in Oregon. She's not a letter writer, but I'm sure she's fine.

Lulu: Is Pete there?

Elenore: Pete's not here right now. He's doing the laundry.

Lulu: What's my son doing?

Elenore: The laundry.

Lulu: Oh. My poor baby.

Elenore: Excuse me?

Lulu: Nothing. What's Doug doing now?

Elenore: He's buying groceries.

Lulu: And what about you? What are you doing?

Elenore: I'm doing the taxes.

Lulu: You're doing the taxes! That's a man's job!

Exercise A.3 (Student Book, page 113)

Look at the picture. Listen and complete the sentences. Use the affirmative or negative of the present progressive.

Doug is at the fruit and vegetable store. He's buying a pineapple. Four people are standing in line. He isn't watching the storekeeper. The storekeeper is cheating Doug. The storekeeper is weighing the pineapple, but he is adding two of his fingers to the weight on the scale.

Exercise C.1 (Student Book, page 121)

Listen and read the conversation. Then answer the questions.

Elenore: What are you doing Pete?

Pete: What am I doing? I'm cooking.

Elenore: Yes, I know. But **what** are you cooking?

Pete: I'm making two chickens with mushrooms and onions and a meatloaf with rice.

Elenore: You're cooking for an army! Who are you cooking for?

Pete: I'm cooking for Caroline, Ray, Andrea, Billy, and us.

Elenore: But why?

Pete: The dinner party.

Elenore: What dinner party?

Pete: Our dinner party.

Elenore: Our dinner party is next week.

Pete: No, it isn't. Look at the calendar. It's tonight.

Elenore: Oh, you're right. Is everything ready?

Pete: Are you kidding? Roll up your sleeves.

Elenore: Yes, sir.

Exercise C.4 (Student Book, page 123)

Doug is returning home. He meets his friend, Noah. Noah is wearing head-phones. Listen and complete their conversation.

Doug: Hi, Noah. What are you doing?

Noah: I'm listening to the ball game.

Doug: Who's playing?

Noah: The Mets are playing the Dodgers.

Doug: Where are they playing?

Noah: In Los Angeles.

Doug: Who's winning.

Noah: It's a tie score. It's the bottom of the ninth inning. Wait. . . . The fans are shouting.

Doug: What's happening?

Announcer: It's a home run.

Noah: Yea! The Mets are winning!

Exercise C.5 (Student Book, page 124)

Elenore is sick. Pete is calling her. Listen to their conversation. Then listen again and answer the questions.

Pete: Hi, Elenore. How are you? How is your cold?

Elenore: Hi, I'm okay now.

Pete: You sound okay. What are you doing?

Elenore: I'm watching TV.

Pete: What are you watching?

Elenore: *(laughing)* An old "I Love Lucy" show.

Pete: What's so funny?

Elenore: *(laughing)* Lucy and her friend, Ethel, are working in a chocolate factory. Lucy isn't working fast enough. She's eating the chocolates and putting them in her pockets. She's making a big mess. It's very funny.

Pete: Lucy is great medicine. Are you taping the program for me? *(sneezing)*

Elenore: Why? You're not a Lucy fan.

Pete: Yes, but I'm catching a cold.

Elenore: *(laughing)* I'll speak to you later.

Exercise D.1 (Student Book, page 127)

Listen and read the letter from Carol to her parents. Underline the verbs in the present progressive.

Dear Mom and Dad,

Thanks for the money. I'm wearing my new sweater today. It's beautiful.

School is wonderful. I'm learning a lot. Yoko, my roommate, is teaching me Japanese cooking. I'm also learning tennis from Dan. Dan is gorgeous! I'm meeting many new people.

My courses are difficult. I'm taking four courses: art, English, American history, and math. I'm doing well in art. I'm doing so-so in English and math. I'm not doing well in history. Actually, at this point, I'm failing it. But grades aren't everything, are they?

Thanks again for the money. I love you both.

Carol

UNIT 6:

INTRODUCTION (STUDENT BOOK, PAGE 134)

Doug and his mother, Elenore, are shopping for clothes. Listen and read their conversation.

Doug: Mom, look at that University of Michigan sweatshirt. I love blue and gold. They're my favorite colors.

Elenore: It's nice, but you have a lot of sweatshirts. You're wearing a nice one right now.

Doug: This sweatshirt is too small. My friends wear big, loose ones. They always buy large or extra-large sweatshirts.

Elenore: But that blue and gold sweatshirt is very expensive. How about this red one? It costs half as much.

Doug: Oh, yuck. This one doesn't have a college name on it. I want a college sweatshirt.

Elenore: Doug, look at these nice shirts. You really need a long-sleeved shirt and dress shoes.

Doug: I don't need a long-sleeved shirt. I have one and I have dress shoes, too. Besides, I hate dress shoes.

Elenore: Your long-sleeved shirt has a big stain on it, and your dress shoes are tight on you.

Doug: My tie covers the stain, and my shoes are okay because I don't wear socks with them.

Elenore: No socks!

Doug: It's the style. The kids at school don't wear socks.

Salesperson: Do you need help?

Doug: Yes, I'm looking for a University of Michigan sweatshirt. Do you have an extra large one?

Elenore: And he needs a shirt and shoes, too.

Salesperson: Well, we have University of Michigan sweatshirts in all sizes. College sweatshirts are very popular this year. They're warm and comfortable, too. Everyone is wearing them.

Doug: See, Mom?

Salesperson: And we have a big sale on long-sleeved shirts and dress shoes.

Elenore: See, Doug?

Exercise A.2 (Student Book, page 137)

Underline the verb or verbs in each sentence. Then listen to the sentences.
Check (✓) each verb that has two syllables.

1. I miss my girlfriend and she misses me.
2. I play tennis and my husband plays golf.
3. I watch the news at six o'clock, but my brother watches the news at seven.
4. Elenore and Pete live in an apartment. Pete's brother lives in a house.
5. Mr. Smith and Mr. Brown coach the boys' tennis team. Ms. Winston coaches the girls' tennis team.
6. Sometimes Doug takes the bus to school. Sometimes Doug and Noah take the subway.
7. I fix lamps. He fixes TVs.
8. Elenore drinks coffee. Pete drinks tea.
9. Norma washes her clothes on Sunday. Carol and Yoko wash their clothes on Tuesday.
10. I wish you a happy birthday, and Pete wishes you a happy birthday, too.
11. Our car needs gas. It needs oil, too.
12. I drive a car. He drives a truck.

Exercise A.3 (Student Book, page 138)

Listen to the sentences and underline the verb in each sentence. Then listen to
the final sound of each verb. Check the sound you hear.

1. He wears T-shirts.
2. He misses his girlfriend.
3. She plays tennis every week.
4. It rains a lot in April.
5. She drinks coffee in the morning.
6. It takes an hour to get to school.
7. He washes his clothes on Sunday.
8. She lives in Boston.
9. He worries about his family.
10. He works at a bank.

Exercise A.5 (Student Book, page 139)

*Listen and complete the conversation. Use **have, don't have,** or **'s**.*

Doug: Mom, I have a headache.

Elenore: Oh, that's too bad.

Doug: I have a stomachache, too.

Elenore: Oh, that's terrible.

Doug: And I have an earache.

Elenore: Stay in bed and rest.

Doug: You mean . . . no school?

Elenore: You silly boy. There's no school today. It's Veteran's Day.

Doug: What?

Elenore: You don't have school today. School's closed. It's a school holiday.

Doug: Gee, Mom. My headache is almost gone. My stomach doesn't hurt, and I don't have an earache anymore.

Exercise B.4 (Student Book, page 148)

*Doug is leaving for school. Listen to the conversation between Doug and his mother. Then answer the questions with **Yes, he does, No, he doesn't,** or **I don't know.***

Doug: Bye, Mom.

Elenore: Bye, Doug. Have a good day at school.

Doug: Thanks, Mom.

Elenore: Doug, do you have your keys?

Doug: Yes, I do.

Elenore: Do you have your lunch?

Doug: Of course I do.

Elenore: Do you have your soccer shoes?

Doug: Of course.

Elenore: Do you have your bookbag?

Doug: Oops!

Exercise C.2 (Student Book, page 154)

Listen and read about Doug's mornings.

A Night Owl

Doug's a "night owl." He hates to get up in the morning. On weekends and vacations, he goes to bed after 1:00 A.M. and gets up after 11:00. Unfortunately for Doug, school starts at 8:15, and Doug needs to get up early. At 7:00, Doug's alarm rings. He wakes up, but he doesn't get up. He stays in bed and day-dreams. At 7:20, Elenore comes in. She has a big smile on her face. She's cheerful and full of energy. She always says, "Dougie, it's time to get up." Elenore is a morning person. Even on vacations, Elenore gets up at 7:00. Doug moans and groans. He's a grouch in the morning. He says, "Go away. Leave me alone. I'm tired. It's early. I need more sleep." Finally, at 7:30, Doug gets up. He jumps out of bed, showers, and gets dressed. At 7:40, he drinks a big glass of orange juice, takes a donut, and runs to the bus stop.

Exercise D.1 (Student Book, page 160)

*Elenore is cleaning a closet. Listen and read the conversation. Underline **this, that, these,** and **those**.*

Elenore: Pete, please look at the clothes in this box. I want to throw away a few things. Our closet is very full.

Pete: Okay. *(Pete looks at the clothes.)* Elenore! This is my favorite sweater. Don't throw it away.

Elenore: That old thing? You never wear it, and it has a big stain.

Pete: I like it.

Elenore: Okay. Anything else?

Pete: Yes. Keep these shoes and these pants.

Elenore: Why? Those shoes are tight, and those pants are short.

Pete: Doug wants them.

Elenore: No, he doesn't.

Pete: I want them.

Elenore: Okay. Anything else?

Pete: Yes, I want this old hat. I know I don't wear it. I know it has a hole and a few stains, but it has some wonderful memories.

Elenore: Okay. You win. Let's get a new closet.

Pete: That's a good idea. Now put everything back in the closet.

Exercise E.2 (Student Book, page 166)

Listen and read the conversation. Cross out the word **one**. *Write the word it replaces.*

Elenore: Doug, where's your new sweatshirt?

Doug: Dino has it. I have his sweatshirt.

Elenore: Why?

Doug: Sometimes Dino and I trade clothes. See, Mom, this is Dino's sweatshirt.

Elenore: But that *one* doesn't have a college name on it.

Doug: I know.

Elenore: And that *one* is small.

Doug: Yes, but Mom, look at it. This *one* has a hood. Hoods are really in style now.

Elenore: Oh.

UNIT 7:

INTRODUCTION (STUDENT BOOK, PAGE 174)

Yoko and Carol are arguing. Listen and read their conversation.

Carol: Yoko, what are you doing?

Yoko: I'm cleaning.

Carol: But you're moving my clothes and my papers.

Yoko: That's because you always leave your clothes and your papers on my desk.

Carol: What are you talking about? Sometimes I leave my clothes on your chair, and once in a while I put my papers or clothes on your desk, but . . .

Yoko: Carol, look at my desk. All your papers, your dirty blue socks, and your gray sweatshirt are on it.

Carol: First of all, those socks aren't mine. They're Dan's. And how often do you leave your books on my desk?

Yoko: Almost never, but you leave your clothes and books on my chair and desk almost every day.

Carol: In my opinion, an empty desk goes with an empty mind.

Yoko: That's nonsense. We need to keep the apartment clean. It looks wonderful when it's clean.

Carol: It looks unnatural.

Yoko: No, it doesn't.

Carol: Yes, it does. *(Yoko goes to the door.)* Where are you going?

Yoko: Out.

Exercise A.2 (Student Book, page 178)

Listen and read Carol's letter to her grandmother:

Dear Grandma Lulu,

Thanks for the delicious Florida oranges and grapefruits. It's so nice of you to send me a surprise every month. My roommate and I have an orange with our breakfast and a grapefruit with our dinner. The fruit is always wonderful, but my roommate, Yoko, isn't. She is sometimes a pest.

Yoko complains because I don't clean the apartment every day. But I do other things for us. I walk Rocky, our dog, every morning and evening. I take out the garbage in the evening, and I go to the supermarket every Monday.

It isn't always easy to share an apartment!

I hope you're fine and enjoying the Florida sunshine. It's cloudy and gray here today, but people in Oregon say, "Don't be upset about Oregon's weather. It always changes."

I look forward to seeing you soon. Say hi to Bertha for me.

Love, Carol.

Now answer the questions. Use the frequency expressions in the box.

Exercise A.7 (Student Book, page 182)

Carol is talking to her mother on the telephone. Complete the conversation. Use the simple present tense or the present progressive. Put the adverbs of frequency in the correct place. Then listen to the conversation and check your work.

Elenore: Hello.

Carol: Hi, Mom.

Elenore: Hi, Carol. It's so good to hear your voice. How are you?

Carol: I'm fine. I'm really working hard these days. I have a tutor in history. Every Thursday he gives me a history lesson.

Elenore: That's good.

Carol: I'm calling about something else.

Elenore: What's the problem?

Carol: My roommate. Yoko always says, "Carol, let's clean the apartment." She cleans the apartment every day. She polishes the furniture twice a week. Right now she's washing the windows.

Elenore: What about you?

Carol: Well, I rarely hang up my clothes, and sometimes I leave some papers on her desk. I never make my bed. It's a waste of time. And I like to live this way.

Elenore: Gee, Carol. You have a problem!

Exercise B.4 (Student Book, page 188)

Complete the conversations. Use the simple present tense or the present progressive. Put the adverbs of frequency in the correct place. Then listen and check your work.

1. **Ron:** Is that you Norma? Your hairdo is different.

   Norma: I'm wearing a wig. Do you like it?

   Ron: Oh, yeah. It's great.

2. **Elenore:** Hello.

   Norma: Hi, Mom. How are you and Dad?

   Elenore: Fine.

   Norma: Is Dad making dinner now?

   Elenore: Not today. He usually prepares a big dinner on Sunday, but he isn't making dinner today.

   Norma: Why not?

   Elenore: There's a new Italian restaurant on the corner. We want to try it.

   Norma: That's nice. Have a good time.

3. **Carol:** Look at Yoko. I really don't understand her. She's washing the curtains again.

   Friend: Does she always wash the curtains?

   Carol: Yes. She washes them almost every week.

4. **Pete:** It's three o'clock. Why are Derek and Ron leaving work?

   Secretary: Tomorrow is a holiday, and they want to get home early.

   Pete: Oh.

5. **Carol:** Why is John wearing a suit and tie today? He almost always wears jeans and a T-shirt. Why is John eating steak and salad? He usually has a hamburger and french fries. And why is John carrying those packages?

   Yoko: I don't know. Let's go ask him.

   Carol: Hi, John. What's up? Why are you wearing that suit to school? Why are you eating that expensive steak? And what's in that box?

   John: Don't you know? Today is my twenty-first birthday. These are presents from some of my friends. Do you and Yoko have a present for me?

Exercise D.1 (Student Book, page 197)

It's a rainy day in Oregon. Yoko, Carol, and Nancy are leaving the school library. Listen and read the conversation. There are five possessive pronouns. Underline them. Above each possessive pronoun write the words it replaces.

Nancy: Excuse me, but I think that's mine.

Carol: What?

Nancy: That yellow umbrella in your bag. It's mine.

Carol: It's not yours.

Nancy: It's not?

Carol: No, it's hers.

Nancy: Whose?

Carol: Yoko's.

Nancy: Yoko's?

Carol: Yes, there she is. Yoko, this is your umbrella, isn't it?

Yoko: Yes. Ah, wait. No, it's not. Mine is right here under this chair. It's exactly the same umbrella.

Carol: Oh, Nancy. I'm so sorry.

Nancy: That's okay. Yoko, you have great taste in umbrellas.

Yoko: Thanks. So do you.

Exercise D.4 (Student Book, page 198)

*Complete the conversaton. Use **you, your, mine,** and **yours.** Then listen and check your work.*

Doug is smiling. It's six-thirty in the morning and he's sleeping. He's dreaming. This is Doug's dream.

Doug: What are these?

Dad: The keys to your new red sports car.

Doug: Mine?

Mom: Yes, yours. It's a present for you on your eighteenth birthday.

Doug: Oh, wow! Are you sure?

Dad: Of course. Every young man needs a sports car.

Doug: You're so right!

UNIT 8:

INTRODUCTION (STUDENT BOOK, PAGE 206)

Carol is visiting San Francisco. She is talking on the phone to her mother, Elenore, in New York. Listen and read their conversation.

Elenore: Hello.

Carol: Hi, Mom.

Elenore: Hi, Carol. Gee, we really miss you.

Carol: I miss you, too.

Elenore: How's San Francisco? When did you and Yoko arrive?

Carol: We arrived late Wednesday night. San Francisco's great. Yesterday we took a sight-seeing bus all around the city. Then we rode on a cable car and walked around Fisherman's Wharf. We had a great time. What about you and Dad? Did you have a nice Thanksgiving?

Elenore: Well, Uncle Bob and Aunt Valerie invited us for dinner.

Carol: How was it?

Elenore: Dinner was delicious. Aunt Valerie made a huge turkey. I brought cranberry sauce, Norma baked a pumpkin pie, and Dad prepared pumpkin curry soup.

Carol: Pumpkin curry soup? That's different. How did it taste?

Elenore: I liked it, but Uncle Bob didn't like it at all. He tried one spoonful and shouted, "Fire!" Then he drank four glasses of water.

Carol: Poor Uncle Bob!

Elenore: Poor Dad! After dinner Uncle Bob turned on the TV and watched a football game. As you know, Dad hates football.

Carol: Did you stay long?

Elenore: No, we left early.

Carol: Well, that was a good idea. Remember last summer when we went to Massachusetts with Aunt Valerie and Uncle Bob. Uncle Bob and Dad had that big fight . . .

Elenore: Please, Carol, don't remind me. Well, I hope you and Yoko enjoy the rest of your vacation.

Carol: Thanks, Mom. I'll call you next week. Bye.

Elenore: Bye.

Exercise A.2 (Student Book page 210)

Now listen to the sentences. Then listen again and check the final sound of each verb.

1. I'm sorry I'm late. I missed my train.
2. The plane arrived on time.
3. Last night she visited her uncle in the hospital.
4. He cooked hot cereal yesterday morning.
5. I'm tired. Yesterday I walked up a lot of hills in San Francisco.
6. Last year she wanted to live in the city, but now she likes the country.
7. We baked a delicious cake yesterday afternoon.
8. Last night I watched a good movie on TV.
9. Uncle Bob joked about Dad's pumpkin curry soup.
10. Everybody hugged and kissed me at my graduation.

Exercise B.4 (Student Book, page 219)

Now complete the story. Use the past tense of the regular and irregular verbs in parentheses. Then listen to the story and check your work.

You Never Know What Will Happen

A long time ago, there lived a poor Chinese peasant. One day a beautiful horse appeared. When the peasant's friends saw the horse, they said, "How lucky you are!"

The peasant responded, "You never know what will happen." After two days, the horse ran away. The peasant's friends came and said, "What a terrible thing. How unlucky you are! The fine horse ran away." The peasant didn't get excited. He simply said, ""You never know what will happen."

Exactly one week later, the horse returned. And it brought three other horses. When the peasant's friends saw the horses, they said to their friend, "Oh. You are so lucky. You now have four horses to help you." The peasant looked at them and once again said, "You never know what will happen."

The next morning the peasant's oldest son was in the field. Suddenly one of the horses ran into him and the boy fell to the ground. He was badly hurt. He became crippled. Indeed, this was terrible, and many people came to the peasant and expressed their sorrow for his son's misfortune. But the peasant simply said, "You never know what will happen."

A month after the son's accident, soldiers rode into the village. They shouted, "There are problems along the border. We are taking every healthy young man to fight." The soldiers took every other young man, but they didn't take the peasant's son. Every other young man fought in the border war, and every man died. But the peasant's son lived a long and happy life. As his father said, you never know what will happen.

Exercise C.1 (Student Book, page 223)

Listen and read about Thanksgiving. Then match the questions with the short answers.

In 1620 a group of people came to America from England. They were the Pilgrims. They left England because the king of England didn't permit them to practice their religion.

The Pilgrims wanted to sail to Virginia and join the first English settlers. But their boat landed to the north, in Massachusetts.

Massachusetts has a cold climate, and the Pilgrims had a difficult time. But with the help of friendly Native Americans, they learned to hunt and grow food in this new area.

After a year the Pilgrims gathered their first harvest. They celebrated with a big feast. They invited the Native Americans to this feast, which lasted for three days.

Today people in the United States still celebrate Thanksgiving. They still eat native American foods like turkey, cranberries, and sweet potatoes, and they give thanks for what they have.

Exercise D.2 (Student Book, page 228)

Last week the students in Al Brown's English class told stories they heard as children. Maria told the class a story from the Bible. Listen and read the story. Then answer the questions.

The Real Mother

Solomon was a king of Israel. He lived about 3,000 years ago. Everyone came to King Solomon with problems because he was very wise.

One day two women approached King Solomon. One carried a baby. The first woman said, "We live in the same house and had our babies three days apart. Her baby died in the night and she changed it for mine. This baby is really mine."

King Solomon turned to the other woman. She said, "No! That woman is lying. That's my baby." The two women started shouting.

King Solomon said, "Stop fighting." He turned to his guard and said, "Get your sword and chop the baby in two. Give one part to this woman and the other to that one." The guard pulled out his sword. As he was about to divide the baby, the first woman screamed, "Stop! Give her the baby. But please don't kill it."

King Solomon then said, "Now I know the true mother. Give the baby to the woman who has just spoken."

UNIT 9:

INTRODUCTION (STUDENT BOOK, PAGE 237)

Pete Winston is talking to his seventy-three-year-old mother, Lulu, on the telephone. Pete lives in New York City. His mother lives in Florida. It's Tuesday morning. Listen and read their conversation.

Lulu: Hello.

Pete: Hi, Mom.

Lulu: Pete, how are you?

Pete: Fine. How are you?

Lulu: I'm wonderful. How are my grandchildren? Is Carol still dating Dan?

Pete: Yes, she is. The kids are okay. But, Mom, where were you last night? I tried calling you until midnight. I was very worried.

Lulu: I'm sorry. I was out. First I went to a wonderful new Japanese restaurant. Then I went to the movies. The food was delicious, and the movie was very funny.

Pete: Oh, that's really nice. Were you with Bertha?

Lulu: No.

Pete: Were you alone?

Lulu: No, I wasn't.

Pete: Who were you with?

Lulu: James Belmont.

Pete: James Belmont! He's a ladies' man. He's not for you. How could you go out with him?

Lulu: Pete! Calm down. He's thoughtful and intelligent.

Pete: But, Mom, he's a little young for you.

Lulu: Good-bye, dear.

Pete: Wait, I'm sorry. . . .

(Lulu hangs up)

Pete: I don't understand Mom. What's she doing?

Exercise A.1 (Student Book, page 240)

Pete is talking to his mother again. Listen and read their conversation.

Lulu: Hello.

Pete: Mom, hi.

Lulu: Pete! It's one o'clock in the morning. What's wrong?

Pete: Nothing's wrong here. But you weren't home all evening.

Lulu: I was at a party.

Pete: Were you with James?

Lulu: Yes. The party was a surprise. It was for a friend of James's.

Pete: Mom, I don't think James is the man for you.

Lulu: Yes, dear.

Pete: I'm serious. You were out with James the last two nights.

Lulu: I know. Do you want to speak with James? He's here now.

Pete: What? Please, Mom. Take care of yourself.

Lulu: Don't worry. Good-bye, dear.

Pete: Bye, Mom!

Pete *(to Elenore)*: Now, I'm really upset. I want to speak to my friend, Milt, the detective.

Elenore: Let's wait.

*Now listen again. There are six sentences with **was, were**, or **weren't**. Write the sentences.*

Exercise A.4 (Student Book, page 242)

Bertha and Lulu are talking on the phone. Bertha feels bad. She bought a sweater she can't wear. Listen and complete their conversation.

Lulu: Hello.

Bertha: Hi, Lulu. It's me, Bertha.

Lulu: Oh, hi. How's everything?

Bertha: Okay. How about you?

Lulu: Oh, James and I had a wonderful time at Epcot Center yesterday.

Bertha: That's nice. I'm really annoyed.

Lulu: Why?

Bertha: I just threw away fifteen dollars.

Lulu: How?

Bertha: I bought a new blue sweater. It was on sale for fifteen dollars. I wore it home because I was cold. After a few minutes, my back and arms began to itch. Red spots appeared on my body. I brought the sweater back to the store.

Lulu: Did you return it?

Bertha: I told the salesperson my problem. He said, "Sorry, no returns on final sales." I made a fuss, but the salesperson repeated, "Sorry, no returns on final sales." I felt terrible. I spent fifteen dollars on the sweater. I was very angry. I threw the sweater at the salesperson. It hit him in the face. He just laughed and said, "Sorry. No returns on final sales."

Lulu: What a story!

Excercise B.1 (Student Book, page 247)

Bekir is asking his teacher about a picture on the classroom wall. Listen and read the conversation.

Bekir: Who's that man in the picture on the wall?

Al Brown: That's the president of the United States.

Bekir: Not that picture. The other picture. Who's the man with the funny white hair?

Al Brown: That's George Washington. He's wearing a wig. Wigs were the style in the 1700s.

Bekir: Who was Washington?

Al Brown: He was the first president of the United States.

Yolanda: Where was he from?

Yoko: He was born in Virginia.

Bekir: When was he born?

Al Brown: He was born in 1732. He became the commander-in-chief of the Continental Army during the American Revolution.

Bekir: What was the war about?

Al Brown: It was a war for independence from Great Britain.

Yoko: Was George Washington a good leader?

Al Brown: Yes, he was. He surprised the British army many times. And he was a good example for his soldiers. He stayed with his men during the bad times—like the long, cold winter at Valley Forge. The war lasted a long time, but finally the British surrendered.

Bekir: How long did the war last?

Al Brown: Eight years. Washington was a great leader, but his army was untrained.

Bekir: Why was the army untrained?

Al Brown: The men were not professional soldiers. They were farmers, traders, lawyers, grocers, hunters, and thieves. But they fought for their homes and won at last. George Washington was elected president in 1789, and he was the president until 1797.

Exercise B.2 (Student Book, page 249)

Carol and Yoko are home from school. Listen to their conversation. Then fill in the blanks with the questions in the box.

Carol: Hi, Yoko. How were your classes today?

Yoko: Okay. Al Brown's class was very interesting.

Carol: What was it about?

Yoko: It was about George Washington.

Carol: That's nice. Any mail?

Yoko: There's a letter for you. I think it's from your mother.

(Carol reads the letter and laughs.)

Yoko: What's so funny.

Carol: My Grandma Lulu has a boyfriend, and my father is worried. I have to call home.

(Carol calls her mother.)

Elenore: Hello.

Carol: Hi, Mom. How's everything? How's Grandma?

Elenore: She's fine, I think.

Carol: Tell me about her boyfriend. What's his name?

Elenore: James Belmont.

Carol: Who is he?

Elenore: Grandma's photography teacher. Dad knows him. They were members of the same photography club twenty years ago. Grandma Lulu and James were away for a couple of days last week.

Carol: No kidding! Where were they?

Elenore: Epcot Center. Dad was really upset.

Carol: Why was he so upset?

Elenore: I'm not sure.

Carol: Well, I think it's wonderful for Grandma to get out.

Elenore: You're probably right.

Exercise C.1 (Student Book, page 254)

Yolanda, a student in Al Brown's English class, looks very upset. Al Brown is talking to her. Listen and read their conversation.

Al Brown: Yolanda, is everything okay?

Yolanda: Not really. There was an earthquake in my hometown yesterday afternoon.

Al Brown: Is your family okay?

Yolanda: I don't know. All the telephone lines were busy last night.

Al Brown: I'm so sorry.

Yolanda: The earthquake wasn't too powerful, but I'm still very worried.

Yoko: Was this the first earthquake in your town, or were there others?

Yolanda: There was one about two years ago. We were lucky. Nobody was hurt.

Al Brown: There was a terrible earthquake in San Francisco a few years ago.

Yolanda: I know. There was another bad earthquake in San Francisco many years ago.

Al Brown: Yes, that's right. There was one in 1989 and another in 1906. In 1989 there were at least 59 deaths and 3,000 injuries. In 1906 there were between 800 and 1,000 deaths.

Bekir: Hey, look at the picture of George Washington. It's shaking.

Yoko: Stop kidding, Bekir. You're impossible!

WRAP IT UP (STUDENT BOOK, PAGE 259)

Elenore is calling her mother-in-law, Lulu, in Florida. Listen and complete their conversation. Use **there is, there are, there was, there were, they are,** *and* **their***.*

Lulu: Hello.

Elenore: Hello, Lulu. This is Elenore.

Lulu: Elenore. What a surprise!

Elenore: Lulu, Pete and I are really worried about you. Just yesterday there was an article in our newspaper about a con man in Florida. There are so many dishonest people. Who is James? What's going on?

Lulu: James is a wonderful, handsome, exciting man.

Elenore: But is he honest?

Lulu: Listen, Elenore. James isn't my boyfriend, and he isn't trying to take my money. He's my business partner.

Elenore: Your business partner?

Lulu: Yes. We're partners in a new business called "Trips for Seniors." There are hundreds of lonely senior citizens in southern Florida. We take them to different places. We provide door-to-door service. You know, there are buses in Florida, but they are often slow. Many senior citizens are afraid to drive at night. Their eyesight isn't so good. And they are afraid to go out alone at night. Last year there were a few muggings in our community at night, and most of the victims were senior citizens.

Elenore: Lulu, your business sounds exciting.

Lulu: It is. Before, I was lonely and tired all the time. Now I feel alive.

Elenore: Lulu, I'm really happy for you.

Lulu: Thanks. Now tell your wonderful husband there is nothing to worry about. I'm just fine.

UNIT 10:

INTRODUCTION (STUDENT BOOK, PAGE 265)

Carol and Yoko are preparing for a party. Listen and read their conversation.

Carol: Who's there?

Bekir: It's Bekir.

Carol: Hi, Bekir. You're very early. The party's at 8:00.

Bekir: I know. I came to help. I can't cook, but I can go shopping for you. I have my car.

Carol: Oh, Bekir. That's so nice of you. There wasn't enough time for us to get everything. Yoko is borrowing some chairs from Maria. Could you get us a few things at the supermarket?

Bekir: Sure. What would you like?

Carol: We need a lot of soda, some potato chips, a little sour cream, some tuna fish, and sugar.

Bekir: Do you have enough ice?

Carol: I don't know. Please get a bag of ice, okay?

Bekir: Sure. How much soda do you need?

Carol: A lot. Get five big bottles, please.

Bekir: And how many bags of potato chips?

Carol: Two bags.

Bekir: How much sour cream?

Carol: A pint.

Bekir: How much tuna fish?

Carol: Three cans are enough.

Bekir: And how much sugar?

Carol: A small box of sugar.

(Bekir returns an hour later.)

Bekir: Here you are. I couldn't get a small box of sugar, so I bought a large one.

Carol: That's fine, but there is a small problem, Bekir. This is tuna for cats.

Bekir: Oh, no.

Yoko: That's okay. I can return it.

Bekir: I feel sick.

Yoko: Why? You didn't eat it.

Bekir: Not today, but my roommate and I always eat this tuna!

Exercise A.5 (Student Book, page 270)

*Complete the conversations with **a few** or **a little**. Then listen and check your answers.*

1. **Yolanda:** Juan has only a few friends at school.

   Luís: I know. But in Mexico he has a lot of friends.

2. **Children:** Just give us a little more time, Mom. We're almost ready.

   Mother: Okay.

3. **Yoko:** Do we need a lot of apples for the cake?

   Carol: No, just a few.

4. **Elenore:** Is there a lot of snow on the ground?

   Pete: No, just a little.

5. **Carol:** Do you have a lot of relatives in California?

Yoko: No, just a few.

6. **Dan:** Last night we studied a little history and a little math.

    Yoko: Then what did you do?

    Dan: We listened to a few tapes.

7. **Mother:** The baby is hungry. Please give her a little milk.

    Father: Okay.

8. **Peter:** Doug ate everything. There's only a little rice left.

    Elenore: That's okay. There's more food in the kitchen.

9. **Carol:** It rained a few days this week. Now the grass looks beautiful.

    Yoko: The grass looks beautiful, but the roads are terrible.

Exercise B.1 (Student Book, page 275)

Carol baked an apple pie for the party. Yolanda asks for the recipe. Listen to their conversation. Then listen again and circle the correct amounts.

Yolanda: Mmm. This pie is delicious, Carol. Did you bake it?

Carol: Yes. It was very easy.

Nancy: Really, how did you make it?

Carol: Well, for the crust, I used two and a half cups of flour, a cup of oil, a quarter of a cup of water . . .

Yolanda: Wait a second . . . I got two and a half cups of flour. What else did you use?

Carol: A cup of oil.

Yolanda: Okay.

Carol: A quarter of a cup of water.

Yolanda: Got it.

Carol: A pinch of salt.

Yolanda: A pinch? What's that? *(Carol pinches Yolanda.)* Ouch!

Carol: That's a pinch. It means a small amount you pinch between two fingers.

Yolanda: Oh.

Carol: I also used an egg, to make the outside of the crust shiny. That's all for the crust.

Yolanda: How many apples did you use for the filling?

Carol: Eight. I also used a cup of sugar and two tablespoons of flour.

Yolanda: The pie is delicious. Thanks for the recipe.

Carol: Ouch! Why did you do that?

Yolanda: I'm practicing my pinches.

Exercise C.2 (Student Book, page 283)

It's eight-fifteen. Carol and Yoko are waiting for their friends to come to their party. Listen to their conversation and complete the sentences.

Yoko: How much milk is there?

Carol: Don't worry. There's enough. We have four quarts. Four quarts are probably too much. People don't drink much milk at parties.

Yoko: Are there enough chairs?

Carol: There are only ten, but people don't usually sit at parties. Do we have enough soda? That's important. People always drink a lot of soda at parties.

Yoko: I think we have enough. Bekir bought five bottles, and we had a few in the refrigerator. What about music? Do we have enough tapes?

Carol: Yes. Dan brought us some tapes last night. They're on the table.

Yoko: Is there enough juice?

Carol: Yes. Relax. We have enough food, enough drinks, and enough music.

Yoko: I guess you're right. But now I have a new worry. Do we have enough friends?

Exercise D.2 (Student Book, page 288)

Listen and complete the sentences.
1. Bekir can't cook, but he can sew.
2. Carol can't understand physics, but she can understand psychology.
3. Carol can bake delicious pies, and Yoko can cook delicious Japanese food.
4. Dan can play tennis, but he can't play golf.
5. Dahlia can speak Hebrew, but she can't speak Korean.
6. Jung Hee can draw and sing.
7. Jung Hee can dance, play tennis, and understand physics.
8. Jung Hee can read English newspapers and write English compositions.
9. She just can't speak English.

Exercise D.3 (Student Book, page 289)

*Yoko is talking to Dina. Yoko's dog, Rocky, is nearby. He's scratching his stomach. Listen to the conversation. Then read each sentence and check **That's right, That's wrong,** or **I don't know.***

Dina: So, this is Rocky.

Carol: Yes.

Dina: He's big. My dog, Poopsie, is small, but he's very smart. Poopsie can do many different things.

Yoko: That's nice.

Dina: He can sit. He can roll over. He can dance. He can even talk. Can Rocky do anything special?

Yoko: Of course. Look at him.

Dina: Why? He's just scratching his stomach.

Yoko: That's amazing.

Dina: Why?

Yoko: He only scratches his stomach when someone is lying.

Exercise E.2 (Student Book, page 295)

Listen to this conversation between Yoko and some friends at her party. Then circle the answer that best completes each sentence.

Juan: Oh, Yoko, this is a great party.

Yoko: Thanks, Juan. I'm so glad you're having a good time. Would you like something to eat?

Juan: Oh, no. I can't eat another thing. The sushi was delicious. Can I have the recipe?

Yoko: Of course. How about you, Yolanda? Would you like something to eat?

Yolanda: Is there any sushi left?

Yoko: Absolutely. I prepared enough sushi for an army. How about something to drink? We have a lot of juice and soda.

Yolanda: I'd like some juice, please.

Yoko: Here, help yourself. Dina, are you leaving?

Dina: I'd like to stay longer, but I can't. Would you please get me my coat?

Yoko: There you are, Dina. Bye.

Dina: Bye, Yoko. See you on Monday.

Exercise E.4 (Student Book, page 296)

Pete arrived home from work. Listen to the conversation between Pete and Elenore. Then listen again and circle the answer that best completes the sentence.

Elenore: Hi, Pete. How was work?

Pete: Fine. Anything new here?

Elenore: Doug would like you to help him with his math homework.

Pete: All right.

Elenore: And Valerie called this afternoon. She and Bob would like us to go camping with them next summer.

Pete: Let me think about that.

Elenore: Also, your mom called. She'd like you to call later tonight.

Pete: Okay. Anything else?

Elenore: Yes. I'd like you to sit down, relax, and try my new pasta dish.

Pete: Now that's a request I like.

UNIT 11:

INTRODUCTION (STUDENT BOOK, PAGE 303)

Lulu Winston calls her friend, Bertha Bean. Listen and read their conversation.

Bertha: Hello.

Lulu: Hi, Bertha. It's me, Lulu.

Bertha: Hi, Lulu.

Lulu: Listen, Bertha. There's a photography exhibit today at the Sheraton Hotel. James has some photos in the show. I'd like to go. Are you free this morning?

Bertha: No, I'm sorry. I'm going to see an ear, nose, and throat doctor.

Lulu: What was that?

Bertha: *(louder)* I'm going to see an ear, nose, and throat doctor.

Lulu: Oh. Why? Are you sick?

Bertha: No, I'm getting a hearing aid.

Lulu: What did you say? You're getting a lemonade?

Bertha: *(louder)* Not a lemonade—a hearing aid!

Lulu: Oh, a hearing aid. Why? You're not deaf.

Bertha: No, but I'm a little hard of hearing.

Lulu: What was that? Speak up.

Bertha: *(louder)* I'm a little hard of hearing.

Lulu: No, you're not. These days everyone is whispering. Tell people to speak louder. I do. Don't get a hearing aid.

Bertha: Why not? The new hearing aids are small and comfortable.

Lulu: Really?

Bertha: Yes. I have an idea. Come with me to the doctor. The doctor is very nice. You might want to speak to him. In the afternoon we'll go to the photography show together.

Lulu: Okay. I may want to ask the doctor a few questions. I might have a little hearing problem, too. I'll meet you at the corner at ten-thirty.

Bertha: Fine. And then we'll go to the photography exhibit together.

Exercise A.2 (Student Book, page 309)

Listen to each situation. Circle the answer that describes what you think Lulu and Bertha are probably going to do.

1. It's 12:30. Lulu and Bertha are leaving the doctor's office. They're both hungry.
2. Lulu and Bertha are now at their favorite coffee shop. The coffee shop is crowded. There aren't any free tables. There are two free seats at the counter. They don't want to wait for a table.
3. The waitress is taking Lulu's and Bertha's orders. Lulu is ordering fish and a baked potato. Bertha is having a hamburger and salad. Lulu is on a diet, but Bertha isn't.
4. The waitress was friendly and helpful. The food was delicious.
5. The photography show is a few blocks away. Lulu and Bertha like to walk. It's a beautiful day.

Exercise A.8 (Student Book, page 313)

*Lulu and Bertha are talking on the telephone. Complete their conversation. Use the simple present tense, the present progressive, the simple past tense, and **be going to** for the future. Then listen to the conversation and check your work.*

Lulu: Hello.

Bertha: Hi, Lulu. What are you doing? Is anyone there?

Lulu: No, I'm alone. I'm watching TV.

Bertha: Are you watching anything special?

Lulu: No. It's a repeat. What's new with you? You sound so happy.

Bertha: I am. I met a really nice gentleman last night.

Lulu: Really? Where did you meet him?

Bertha: At Tamar's house. He's a friend of Tamar's cousin.

Lulu: Where is he from?

Bertha: Connecticut. He came to Florida last week. He's looking for an apartment now because he's going to move here next April.

Lulu: When are you going to see him again?

Bertha: Tomorrow night. We're going to go to an Italian restaurant in Key Biscayne.

Lulu: Are you going to take a taxi there?

Bertha: No, he rented a car yesterday.

Lulu: When am I going to meet him?

Bertha: Not too soon.

Lulu: Okay, Bertha. I understand. You don't want competition from me.

Bertha: That's right.

Lulu: Have a wonderful time.

Bertha: Thanks, Lulu. Bye.

Lulu: Bye, Bertha.

Exercise B.1 (Student Book, page 316)

Lulu and Bertha are at the photography exhibit. Listen and read their conversation. Underline the five sentences in the present progressive. Then write the two sentences that use the present progressive for the future.

Bertha: Look at this photograph by James, Lulu.

Lulu: Which one?

Bertha: This one here. An older man is playing chess with a young girl—probably his granddaughter. The man's eyes are very deep and sad. It's a wonderful photograph.

Lulu: Yes, you're right. Look, there's James. He's talking to a group of men.

Bertha: Where?

Lulu: Over there. He's wearing a blue suit and a red tie.

Bertha: Now, I see him.

Lulu: Hi, James.

James: Hello, Lulu. Hello, Bertha. Thanks so much for coming to my show. I'm really excited. My photograph of the man and his granddaughter won first prize. Some reporters are taking me to dinner tonight. We're going to the restaurant in this hotel. After dinner, a photographer from one of the papers is going to take my picture.

Lulu: Congratulations, James. You deserve the first prize. You have a lot of talent.

James: Thanks, Lulu.

Exercise B.2 (Student Book, page 317)

Listen and complete the conversations.

1. **Pete:** Did you listen to the weather forecast?

   Elenore: Yes. We're going to have three to six inches of snow.

   Pete: Really?

   Elenore: Yes.

   Pete: Are you still playing tennis this afternoon?

Elenore: No. I'm staying home and cleaning the apartment.

Pete: That's a good idea.

Elenore: Would you like to help me?

2. **Carol:** Andrea, what are you doing?

   Andrea: I'm cutting Billy's hair.

   Carol: Stop right now. Your mother is going to be very angry.

3. **Lulu:** Where are you going this afternoon? Would you like to go to the beach?

   Bertha: I can't. I'm going to the hairdresser's.

   Lulu: Oh. What's the occasion?

   Bertha: I'm going to a jazz concert tonight.

   Lulu: A jazz concert? What do you know about jazz?

   Bertha: Nothing, but my friend, Ray, is crazy about jazz. He knows all the musicians. He's going to introduce me to them.

   Lulu: Ooh-la-la!

Exercise C.2 (Student Book, page 323)

Tamar Lyman is a member of Lulu Winston and James Belmont's group, "Trips for Seniors." Listen to Tamar's conversation with Lulu. Write the group's activities for tomorrow. Use the phrases in the box.

Tamar: Hi, Lulu. This is Tamar Lyman.

Lulu: Hi, Tamar. What's up?

Tamar: Lulu, I'm going on your trip tomorrow, but I can't find my schedule. Sometimes, I'm so forgetful. I guess I'm getting old.

Lulu: Don't worry about it. Everyone is a little forgetful. Young people are forgetful, too, but nobody notices when a young person forgets. Anyway, this is the schedule for tomorrow. We'll meet at the Star Diner at nine o'clock. You can eat breakfast there or just have a cup of coffee. At about ten we'll leave for Palm Beach. We'll arrive there about eleven o'clock, and we'll shop in Palm Beach for about two hours. There are some wonderful sales in the stores this week. Then we'll stop for lunch. At two o'clock we'll get on the bus to return home. We'll be back home at about three.

Tamar: Thanks a lot, Lulu. I'll see you tomorrow at ten.

Lulu: Not ten, nine.

Tamar: Oh, that's right. I forgot.

Exercise D.2 (Student Book, page 330)

Pete and Elenore are packing for their trip to Oregon and California. Elenore usually travels with very few clothes, but Pete always takes a lot. Listen to their conversation. Then tell why Pete is taking each item.

Elenore: Pete, your suitcase is so heavy. Why are you taking so much?

Pete: I need everything I'm taking.

Elenore: Why are you taking your boots?

Pete: I heard it's beautiful in Crater Lake National Park. We may want to go mountain climbing.

Elenore: Oh, then I may take my boots, too. But why are you taking three sweaters? Two are enough.

Pete: It might get very cold at night.

Elenore: Oh. Why are you taking two watches?

Pete: I might lose one. I can't manage without a watch.

Elenore: And do you really need two cameras?

Pete: Yes. Remember last year our camera broke on the first day of our vacation? We couldn't take any photos.

Elenore: Well, why do you need a hair dryer?

Pete: I may want to dry my hair after a swim.

Elenore: What hair?

UNIT 12:

INTRODUCTION (STUDENT BOOK, PAGE 338)

Elenore and Pete are having dinner. Listen and read their conversation.

Elenore: Pete, did you get my message?

Pete: What message?

Elenore: I called your office this morning. I left a message for you to call home.

Pete: I'm sorry. I never got the message. Was it important?

Elenore: Not really, but that new assistant of yours isn't very good. Bob was much better. The phone rang six times. Bob always answered sooner. Your new assistant has a nice voice, but she wasn't as friendly as Bob, and she spoke too softly for me to hear her.

Pete: That's too bad. She types very quickly and accurately.

Elenore: Did many people apply for the job?

Pete: No, only two. My new assistant, Sally, had more experience and better references than the other person.

(the next evening)

Elenore: You know, Pete, I spoke to Sally again. Today she was much quicker to pick up the phone, much friendlier, and much more confident than yesterday. Did you complain to her?

Pete: No, I didn't. She remembered your call and felt terrible about not telling me.

Elenore: What did you say?

Pete: I said, "Sally, my wife thinks you have a lovely voice. She enjoyed talking with you."

Elenore: What's that expression? You can win more bears with honey. Pete, you're a lot smarter than I am!

Pete: Thanks, Elenore. That's nice to hear.

Exercise A.1 (Student Book, page 342)

Pete's new assistant, Sally, has an eight-year-old son named Steve. Steve is playing with his friend Jimmy at the playground. Complete their conversation. Use the comparative form of the adjectives in the box. Then listen to the conversation and check your work.

Jimmy: Let's race.

Steve: Okay.

(The boys race. Jimmy wins the race.)

Jimmy: I won. I'm faster than you are.

Steve: So? I can lift this rock and you can't. I'm stronger than you are.

Jimmy: See this watch? It cost $100. It's more expensive than your watch.

Steve: So what? My dad is six feet tall and he weighs 200 pounds. He's bigger than your dad.

Jimmy: Well, my mom won a beauty contest in high school. She's prettier than your mom.

Steve: No, she isn't.

Jimmy: Yes, she is. And my mom knows 200 jokes. She's funnier than your mom, too.

Steve: Well, my grandparents give me presents every month. They're richer than your grandparents.

Jimmy: How do you know? Look, there's Ron. Hey, Ron! Do you want to race?

Exercise A.3 (Student Book, page 343)

Last week Pete interviewed Sally Cooper and Gail Finger. Listen to their interviews. Then compare Sally and Gail. Use the adjectives in parentheses.

Sally: Hello. I'm Sally Cooper. I saw your ad in the newspaper. I'd like to work as your assistant.

Pete: Do you have any experience?

Sally: Yes, I worked as a secretary for Hollander and Stram Law Firm for ten years. I have references from Ms. Hollander and Mr. Stram. Here is my resume.

Pete: Thank you. Why did you leave?

Sally: The firm moved to Atlanta, but I didn't want to move. Here in New York I'm closer to my family. I'm a single mother, and my son is happy at his school.

Pete: Can you type?

Sally: Yes. I type 65 words a minute and I can take shorthand.

Pete: When can you begin?

Sally: Next week.

Pete: Well, the salary is a little lower than what you received at Hollander and Stram, but you get a three-week vacation, good health benefits, and a pension.

Sally: The salary is a little low, but the job sounds very good.

Pete: Thank you for coming. I'll call you in a few days.

Sally: Thank you.

Now listen to Pete's interview with Gail.

Pete: Hello.

(Gail chews gum audibly during interview)

Gail: Hi. Is there a job opening?

Pete: Are you applying for the job of assistant to the director?

Gail: Uh-huh.

Pete: What's your name?

Gail: Gail.

Pete: What's your last name?

Gail: Finger.

Pete: Do you have any experience?

Gail: Nope.

Pete: Can you type and take shorthand?

Gail: I can type, but I can't type fast. I can't take shorthand.

Pete: How fast can you type?

Gail: About thirty words a minute. I'm faster when there's loud music.

Pete: Excuse me?

Gail: Just kidding.

Pete: When can you begin?

Gail: Any time.

Pete: Do you have any references?

Gail: Well, I worked as a counselor last summer. I might be able to get a reference from camp.

Pete: Do you have any questions about the job?

Gail: No.

Pete: Well, thanks for applying.

Gail: Bye.

Exercise B.4 (Student Book, page 351)

Listen to the conversation between Elenore and Pete. Then choose the best adverb to complete each sentence.

Elenore: How's your new assistant, Pete?

Pete: I'm really happy with her. She works hard. She types fast and accurately. She takes shorthand quickly. She listens carefully. I have only one problem. She still doesn't take messages well. Last week she said, "Mr. Hen called. He wants to meet you on June second at one o'clock." In fact, Mr. Chen called. He wanted to meet me on July first at two o'clock.

Exercise C.3 (Student Book, page 356)

Sally and her sister, Penny, are at a grocery store. Sally is choosing a honey-dew melon. Listen to their conversation. Then read the sentences. Check **That's right, That's wrong,** *or* **I don't know.**

Penny: Sally, are you ready to leave?

Sally: No, I can't find a good honeydew.

Penny: Why not? Here's a good one.

Sally: No, this one is too small.

Penny: What about this one here?

Sally: No, that one is too big.

Penny: Take that one in the corner. It's the right size.

Sally: You're right, but it's too soft. See, it's overripe.

Penny: Okay. Here. This one is hard.

Sally: It's too hard.

Penny: Sally, what's wrong with you? You're choosing a honeydew, not a husband.

Sally: Well, I'm going to buy this pineapple. It's just right.

Exercise D.2 (Student Book, page 362)

Sally is speaking to her brother Lou. Listen and complete the conversation.

Sally: Lou, what's wrong? You sound very upset.

Lou: I am. I didn't get that promotion.

Sally: Oh, no. Who got it?

Lou: Mary did. I don't understand it. I work as quickly as she does.

Sally: I know. You're both very fast workers.

Lou: I'm as punctual as she is.

Sally: That's right. You never come late.

Lou: I'm as polite as she is, and I'm as talented as she is, too.

Sally: What about her background and experience?

Lou: She has the same background and experience as I do.

Sally: Why do you think they gave her the job?

Lou: I think it's because she's a woman.

Sally: Well, that's a switch. It's usually just the opposite.

Exercise D.4 (Student Book, page 363)

*Listen to the conversation between Dina and Dan. Then read the sentences. Check **That's right** or **That's wrong**.*

Dan: What's wrong, Dina? You look very annoyed.

Dina: I am. I can't understand Bekir. He invited Yolanda to the dance. I expected him to invite me.

Dan: Really?

Dina: Yes, of course. Yolanda isn't as smart as I am.

Dan: Well, she is a very good student, and she seems intelligent to me.

Dina: She isn't as pretty as me.

Dan: Oh?

Dina: She certainly isn't as rich as me.

Dan: Well, I'm not certain about all that, but I am sure of one thing.

Dina: What's that?

Dan: Yolanda isn't as conceited as you.

Exercise E.2 (Student Book, page 368)

Listen and complete the conversations.

1. **Al Brown:** How was registration?

Registrar: Not so good. We had fewer students than last semester.

Al Brown: Spring registration is usually lower.

2. **Noah:** I'm thinking of applying for a part-time job at that restaurant. What do you think?

Doug: Business is bad. I think they're losing money. They have fewer waiters than they had in the past, but you never know.

3. **Carol:** Do you like my new skirt and sweater?

Yoko: Yes, but you need more color. Here, wear my red and blue scarf.

Carol: Thanks.

Yoko: Something is still wrong.

Carol: You're right. I think I'm wearing too much jewelry. I think the sweater will look better with less jewelry. How do I look now?

Yoko: Great.

4. **Pete:** Elenore, would you please taste the salad?

Elenore: Mmm, it's good. It just needs more pepper.

Pete: How is it now?

Elenore: It's better, but it still needs something.

Pete: I'll add some more salad dressing. Now try it.

Elenore: Now it's perfect, but save it for tomorrow.

Pete: Why?

Elenore: I had a huge salad for lunch, and I really don't want any more rabbit food today.

UNIT 13:

INTRODUCTION (STUDENT BOOK, PAGE 375)

It's Sunday morning. Doug and his mother, Elenore, are talking about the night before. Listen and read their conversation.

Doug: Good morning.

Elenore: Good morning, Doug. Did you enjoy the movie last night?

Doug: It was so-so. How about you? Did you and Dad have a nice time at the party?

Elenore: Don't ask.

Doug: Why?

Elenore: We thought that Dad's new boss, Sheila, and her husband, Bob, were having a big party last night. When Dad and I arrived at their house, Sheila was standing in front of a mirror. She was wearing a nightgown and a green facial mask. Bob opened the door. He was wearing pajama bottoms and putting on a T-shirt.

Doug: Oh, no.

Elenore: I was really embarrassed.

Doug: What about Dad? What did he say?

Elenore: He turned to me and said, "Elenore, you didn't tell me it was a costume party."

Doug: Was it a costume party?

Elenore: No. Sheila laughed and said, "Pete, we're not having a costume party, and our party isn't tonight." Then she showed us an invitation. Their party is going to be next Saturday night. We showed up on the wrong day!

Doug: What did you say?

Elenore: I didn't know what to say.

Doug: And Dad?

Elenore: He didn't either. We just said, "Oh, oh, oh."

Doug: Well, does Dad still have a job?

Elenore: Yes, but only because Sheila has a good sense of humor.

Exercise A.2 (Student Book, page 379)

There was a murder last night. The police believe the murder occurred at 7:00 P.M. They are questioning three people: Mr. Smith, Ms. Brown, and Mr. Clapp. Listen to the conversation. Then listen again and write what each person was doing when the murder occurred.

Police: Hello, Mr. Smith. As you know, we have a few questions for you.

Mr. Smith: Certainly. I understand.

Police: Mr. Smith, where were you last night at seven o'clock?

Mr. Smith: I was at the Star Diner. I was eating dinner with two friends.

Police: Can I have their names and phone numbers?

Mr. Smith: Certainly. Here you are.

Police: Thank you, Mr. Smith.

Police: Ms. Brown, we have a few questions for you.

Ms. Brown: I'm innocent. I didn't kill Mr. Rodriguez.

Police: Yes. We just have a few questions. What were you doing last night at seven o'clock?

Ms. Brown: I was driving to my cousin's home in New Jersey.

Police: I see. What time did you arrive there?

Ms. Brown: I don't remember. Wait a second. I paid a toll and kept the receipt. The time is here on my receipt.

Police: Oh, this is helpful. You paid the toll at seven-fifteen.

Ms. Brown: See? I'm innocent.

Police: Yes, well, thank you for coming.

Police: Mr. Clapp, what were you doing at seven o'clock last night?

Mr. Clapp: I was sleeping.

Police: At seven o'clock in the evening?

Mr. Clapp: I wasn't feeling well all day yesterday, so I went to bed early.

Police: Was anyone at home?

Mr. Clapp: No, I live alone.

Police: Well, thank you, Mr. Clapp. Please don't leave town until you hear from us.

Mr. Clapp: Yes, sir.

Exercise A.5 (Student Book, page 381)

*Norma is talking to her father on the telephone. She's telling him how some-
one took her car. Complete the conversation. Use the correct form of the verbs
in parentheses. Then listen to the conversation and check your work.*

Pete: Hello.

Norma: Hi, Dad. How are you?

Pete: Fine.

Norma: Are you busy?

Pete: No, not really. I was just looking at the paper when you called. How are you doing?

Norma: I'm okay, but I'm a little upset. Someone stole my car yesterday.

Pete: Oh, no! How did it happen?

Norma: You're not going to believe my story. Yesterday I was driving home from work when someone in an old car hit my new car. I wasn't hurt, but I got out to check my car. The man in the other car got out of his car, too. I expected to exchange addresses with him. I was walking to his car when he ran over to my car. Then he got in my car and drove away.

Pete: No! I don't believe it. You're joking.

Norma: Unfortunately, I'm serious.

Pete: What did you do then?

Norma: I took his car and went to the police. I gave them my name and address and I described my car to them. Now they're trying to find the thief.

Pete: But you need a car to get to work. You aren't working today or tomorrow, but what are you going to do on Monday?

Norma: While I was returning home from the police station, I met a friend from work. When I told him my story, he offered to lend me his car. He never uses it on weekdays. He's a very nice guy. But I feel ter-rible. I'm usually so careful.

Pete: I know. You are very careful. You always lock your car and never leave the key in your car. What a terrible story!

Norma: Well, I'm going to call the police later today.

Pete: Listen, if there's anything I can do, please let me know. Do you have enough money?

Norma: Yes, Dad. I'm okay. Don't worry. I'll call and let you know what happens.

Pete: Okay. Bye, Norma. Take care of yourself.

Exercise B.6 (Student Book, page 390)

*Saturday night Pete and Elenore got home at 11:00. Pete showed Elenore their
invitation to Sheila's party. Listen to their conversation. Then circle the answer
that best completes the sentence.*

Elenore: Pete, I don't have my reading glasses. Please read the invitation to me.

Pete: It says, "You're invited. Saturday, March 19, 9:30 P.M." The party is next week. I feel terrible.

Sheila's my boss. We owe them an apology.

Elenore: Yes, we do. I'll write them a note.

Pete: Okay, and let's send them some flowers.

Elenore: All right.

Pete: Let's buy them some cookies.

Elenore: If you think so.

Pete: Let's take them out to dinner and maybe get them theater tickets.

Elenore: Let's not overdo it.

Pete: But, Elenore. I saw my boss in her nightgown with green gook all over her face!

Exercise B.7 (Student Book, page 391)

Listen to the conversation between Carol and Yoko. Then read the conversation in your book. There are several differences between the conversation in the book and the one on the tape. Listen again, underline the differences, and write the changes above the lines. Then listen and check your work.

(Background conversation between a male and a female, native speakers of Spanish)

Male: *Hola, María. ¿Qué tal?*

Female: *Muy bien, Juan. ¿Y tú?*

Carol: Yoko, what are you listening to? It doesn't sound like English or Japanese.

Yoko: It isn't. It's a Spanish tape. Maria and Juan gave it to me. They're teaching me Spanish.

Carol: How?

Yoko: Well, first I listen to their tape and repeat each sentence to myself. Then we meet and I say the sentences to them. They correct my pronunciation, and they explain the sentences to me. I'm really learning a lot.

Carol: Are you teaching them Japanese?

Yoko: Next week we're going to begin. I'll say a Japanese sentence to Juan and Maria. Then they'll repeat it to me. Then I'll explain the meaning to them.

Carol: That sounds like fun.

Exercise C.2 (Student Book, page 398)

*Pete and Elenore are getting ready to go bicycle riding in the park. Listen to their conversation. Then answer the questions. Check **Yes**, **No**, or **I don't know**.*

Pete: I'm hot.

Elenore: I am, too. It's about eighty degrees and very humid.

Pete: I'm a little tired.

Elenore: I am, too. I couldn't sleep well last night. The air conditioner wasn't working well.

Pete: I remember. You know, Elenore, I don't really want to go bike riding.

Elenore: I don't, either. Let's go to the movies instead.

Pete: That's a terrific idea.

Exercise D.2 (Student Book, page 403)

Listen and read the conversation. Then complete the questions. Use phrasal verbs.

Doug: Mom, you never told me what happened at Sheila and Bob's house after Sheila said the party was next Saturday.

Elenore: Well, we wanted to leave immediately, but Sheila asked us to stay. She and Bob disappeared. First Sheila took off her mask and put on a beautiful outfit. She returned in five minutes and joined us in the living room. Then she turned off the TV and put away some magazines and papers. She turned on the stereo and brought out some crackers and cheese. We had a great time.

Doug: What about Bob?

Elenore: That was the strange thing. He disappeared and never returned. Dad and I didn't ask about him, and Sheila didn't say anything, either.

Doug: Oh, well. At least Bob's not Dad's boss.

Exercise E.2 (Student Book, page 409)

Complete the story. Use the correct form of the phrasal verbs in the box. Then listen and check your work.

Last Saturday Elenore and Pete were eating out at an Italian restaurant when a woman came in and sat down at the next table. Both Elenore and Pete were surprised because the woman looked very much like Elenore.

Elenore and Pete began talking with the woman, and soon they asked her to join them. She and Elenore discovered several other similarities. Both women grew up in New York City. They both have three children, and they both like spicy food.

When Pete said he'd like to meet the woman's husband, she said, "He'll be here soon. He usually shows up late." Elenore grinned and said, "Just like my Pete."

At that moment, the woman smiled, waved, and said, "There's my Sammy." Pete and Elenore turned. Sammy was six feet tall and had thick blond hair. Pete said, "I guess he's not my twin."

UNIT 14:

INTRODUCTION (STUDENT BOOK, PAGE 417)

Carol, who is in Oregon, is speaking to her parents in New York. Listen to their telephone conversation.

Elenore: Hello.

Carol: Hi, Mom.

Elenore: Hi, Carol. How are you?

Carol: Fine. Listen, Mom. I have some very important news. Is Dad on the extension?

Elenore: No, he's in the kitchen. Should I get him?

Carol: Yes. I have to tell you both something very special.

(pause)

Pete: Hi, Carol. What's up?

Carol: Mom, Dad, you'd better sit down.

Pete: Okay, Carol. Now, what's your important news?

Carol: Mom, Dad, I'm engaged.

Pete: You're what?

Carol: I'm engaged to Dan.

Elenore: That's . . . uh, wonderful, but isn't it sudden?

Carol: Oh, no. We met in October, and we see each other all the time.

Pete: Tell us about Dan.

Carol: He's the most handsome man in the world. His eyes are big and bright. His hair is thick and wavy. His shoulders are very broad, and he has the cutest dimples in the world.

Pete: I'm sure he's gorgeous, but what does he do?

Carol: Oh, he's a poet, and . . .

Pete: *(interrupting)* A poet? But Carol, can a poet earn a living?

Carol: Don't worry, Dad. You have to meet Dan. We're really in love. And I have some more news. You and Mom are going to be . . .

Pete and Elenore: What?

Elenore: Carol? Carol? Pete, we just got cut off! What's going on? What should we do?

Pete: Well, we should call her back. You hang up and I'll try.

Pete to Elenore: Oh, no. Carol's line is busy. Maybe we'd better wait near the phone until she calls back.

Carol to Yoko: Oh, Yoko. I must call my parents right back. We just got disconnected. They think I'm marrying a poet.

Exercise A.2 (Student Book, page 421)

Listen to the conversation between Elenore and Pete. Listen again and complete the conversation.

Elenore: Pete, I'm worried. What should we do? Should we call Dan?

Pete: We don't know his phone number.

Elenore: Call information.

Pete: We don't know his last name. Who should we ask for, "Dan the poet"?

Elenore: Maybe we should fly to Oregon. Carol's so young and innocent. She's just a baby.

Pete: Carol's not so young, and she's probably not so innocent.

Elenore: I think you should call Milt. He lives near Carol. He could visit her.

Pete: Elenore, this isn't like you. You always say, "Trust the children." Well, now we should trust Carol and we shouldn't jump to conclusions. Anyway, let's wait for her to call us back.

Elenore: Well, okay.

Exercise D.1 (Student Book, page 438)

Listen to the conversation between Doug, Elenore, and Pete. Then read the conversation. Underline the superlative adjectives and adverbs.

Elenore: Doug, please don't use the phone now.

Doug: Why not?

Pete: Carol just called and we got cut off. We're waiting for her to call back. We tried to call her back, but the line was busy.

Doug: Well, why do you two look so strange?

Elenore: Carol just told us she's engaged to Dan.

Doug: Oh, I know all about Dan.

Pete: You do? Well, please tell us.

Doug: He's the most handsome guy on campus.

Pete: Do you have any other information?

Doug: He drives the coolest car. He has the biggest and best collection of CDs, and he wears the funkiest clothes.

Elenore: Funky?

Doug: You know, loud and fashionable.

Elenore: That sounds like Dan. How do you know so much? Did you speak to Carol?

Doug: No, but Carol told Dino's sister, and Dino told me.

Pete: Did she happen to say anything more about Dan?

Doug: Oh, yeah, I forgot. He has the cutest dimples in the world.

Pete: Great.

WRAP IT UP (STUDENT BOOK, PAGE 444)

Carol finally calls Pete and Elenore back. Listen and read the conversation.
Then answer the questions.

Elenore: Hello.

Operator: I have a collect call for you from Carol Winston. Do you accept the charges?

Elenore: Yes, yes.

Carol: Hello.

Elenore: Carol! We tried to call you many times. The line was always busy. I'm so glad you reached us. Carol, when we got interrupted, you said Dad and I were going to be something. What was that about?

Carol: Oh . . . Oh, yes. You and Dad are going to be great grandparents. Our dog, Rocky, is going to be a father. But, listen. Before you ask any other questions, let me tell you about Dan and me.

Elenore: I think you'd better explain, because Dad and I are really very concerned.

Carol: Dan's father has the biggest advertising agency in Portland, and Dan is going to work for him. Dan is very creative and writes clever poems and jingles. He writes the most beautiful love poems, too, but they're just for me.

Elenore: Well, that's good to hear. But, what about you? You're twenty years old. This is the nicest time of your life. Today most women want careers. Most women want to finish college and get a profession. You should travel. You should live on your own. You're too young to get married. You're certainly too young to be a parent. Don't you agree?

Carol: Mom, you don't understand. I'm in love. Nothing else matters. Besides, I plan to go to school and work after I'm married.

Elenore: Should I laugh or should I cry?

Carol: Don't laugh or cry. Just buy some extra groceries. I invited Dan to spend a few days with all of us in New York, and he's got a big appetite. Is that okay with you?

Elenore: Of course.

PUTTING IT ALL TOGETHER:

Exercise A.1 (Student Book, page 450)

Pete is talking to his wife, Elenore, on the telephone. He is upset with their teenage son, Doug. Complete the conversation. Choose the correct verb forms and modals. Then listen to the conversation and check your work.

Elenore: Hello.

Pete: Well, finally.

Elenore: Pete?

Pete: Yes, it's me. I finally reached you.

Elenore: What are you talking about?

Pete: I tried to call you at 10:00, at 12:00, and at 2:00. I couldn't reach you. The line was always busy. Was Doug on the phone again?

Elenore: I guess so.

Pete: I don't understand him. Every day he talks to his friends for hours. Yesterday when I asked him a few questions, he answered every question with one word.

Elenore: Many teenagers are like that.

Pete: Well, I wasn't. When I was a teenager, I didn't spend hours on the phone. I went to school. After school I had to work in my father's store. I couldn't go out.

Elenore: But Pete. You always say, "I don't want my children to work as hard as I did."

Pete: I know, but Doug isn't grateful. He's so lucky he doesn't have to work and study at the same time. He doesn't understand that.

Elenore: Not now, but one day in the future he'll understand.

Pete: I guess you're right. Do I sound very old?

Elenore: No, just a little old-fashioned.

Exercise A.2 (Student Book, page 451)

Doug and his friend Noah are talking about their parents. Complete the conversation. Choose the correct verb forms and modals. Then listen to the conversation and check your work.

Noah: What's the matter, Doug? Are you okay?

Doug: I guess so. It's just that sometimes my father and I see things in different ways. My father can't understand me. We live in different worlds. He believes in two things: work and study. I'll never work so much. After college, I'm going to buy a boat. I'm going to enjoy life. How's your mom?

Noah: Sometimes she's just like your dad. What's worse, she still thinks I'm a child. Last Saturday night, I came home a little late. My mom talked about it for two hours. I had to listen to her tell me every horror story about the city at night. Then, the next day my grandma visited us. You know my grandma. Her ideas are very old-fashioned. I think she'd like me to wear a suit and tie to bed. I prefer a more casual look. Well, when she arrived Sunday morning, I was wearing my comfortable old jeans. My grandma was angry that I was wearing jeans. My mom was angry that my jeans had holes in them. I was the angriest of all. I don't think my mom or my grandma should tell me what to wear.

Doug: You're right. You have to show them you're not a child anymore. It's really not easy living with parents.

Noah: You said it!

Exercise A.3 (Student Book, page 452)

Noah's mother, Rita Steiner, is talking to Pete and Elenore. Complete the conversation. Choose the correct verb forms and modals. Then listen to the conversation and check your work.

Pete: Hello.

Rita: Hello, Pete. This is Rita Steiner, Noah's mother. How are you?

Pete: Oh, hi, Rita. I'm fine, thanks. And you?

Rita: Okay, thanks. May I please speak to Elenore?

Pete: Elenore's out now. She'll be back in an hour. Can she call you then?

Rita: Yes. Please ask her to call me.

Pete: Okay. Bye.

Rita: Bye.

Rita: Hello.

Elenore: Hi, Rita? This is Elenore. Is everything okay?

Rita: I guess so, but I need some advice. Lately, Noah and I don't agree on anything.

Elenore: Teenagers are difficult to live with. Just yesterday Doug and Pete had a big fight about the telephone. But you know, Pete and I like Noah a lot. In our house he's always polite and charming.

Rita: Noah? That's wonderful to hear. At home, he's not so charming. In the past Noah was always quiet and well behaved. He listened to me. He did all his school work on time. Now his school work is always late. Before, he wore neat and clean clothes. Now he's seventeen, and I can't recognize him. Last weekend, when my mother visited us, he was wearing jeans with holes all over them. And yesterday he came home two hours late. When I complained, he got angry. Elenore, you have three children. Tell me. What should I do?

Elenore: Would you like to have dinner with us next Saturday night? Doug and Noah are going to a soccer game. We could have dinner and talk about the boys. Pete and I might not have any answers, but with three children, we have a lot of good stories. Then we can look at Noah and Doug's baby pictures and remember the "good old days."

Rita: Elenore, that's a terrific idea. Thanks so much. I'll see you on Saturday.

Exercise A.8 (Student Book, page 455)

Carol invited her boyfriend, Dan, to spend a few days with her in New York. Carol and Dan arrived in New York from their school in Corvallis, Oregon, three days ago. It is 7:00 P.M. They are having dinner with Carol's parents, Elenore and Pete, and Carol's brother, Doug.

Complete the conversation. Use the correct form of each verb in parentheses. Then listen to the conversation and check your work.

Pete: Well, Dan, what do you think of New York?

Dan: I think New York is great. I love the people, the buildings, the stores, and the food. I love everything about it!

Doug: You do? Why?

Dan: It's so alive! Corvallis is a nice small town, but it's too quiet for me. My parents decided I should go to school there because it's clean, safe, and near our family's home and business, but I prefer big cities like New York.

Carol: I don't understand you. I love Corvallis. You know, clean, safe towns are hard to find, and the scenery in Corvallis is beautiful. Also, the people are friendly. Here in New York people are always in a hurry. New Yorkers talk fast. They walk fast. They even eat fast.

Dan: But New York is special!

Elenore: Carol never liked New York, Dan, but I do. In my opinion, it's the greatest city in the world. By the way, what did you two do earlier today?

Dan: First, we walked along Fifth Avenue. After that we went to Rockefeller Center and the Museum of Modern Art. Then we rode the subway. It wasn't too bad.

Doug: Wow! You're brave!

Carol: Doug, don't be so mean and don't eat so much. You're eating all the meat. Leave some for us.

Doug: I'm a growing boy. Look, it's snowing outside.

(Everyone looks outside)

Carol: No, it's not. Hey, Doug, you just took the last potato.

Elenore: Don't worry. There's more food in the kitchen.

Dan: Mrs. Winston, the roast beef is delicious.

Elenore: Thanks, Dan.

Doug: Enjoy it now, Dan. When our sister Norma is here, we usually don't have meat. She's a vegetarian.

Dan: I know. Carol told me.

Doug: Right now Norma is protesting for animal rights. She stops every woman in a fur coat and hands her pictures of dead animals and articles about animal rights.

Elenore: Norma has strong beliefs.

Carol and Doug: We know.

(The telephone rings. Elenore answers the phone)

Elenore: Hello? Hi, Norma. How's everything? What? No! Really? Oh, my!

Pete: What's going on?

Elenore: Norma is going to be on the news later tonight.

Dan: How exciting!

Doug: Well, things are never quiet around here! Maybe the police arrested her and put her in jail.

Elenore: Doug!

Exercise C.1 (Student Book, page 459)

It's Sunday afternoon. Pete is speaking to his mother, Lulu, who lives in Florida. Complete the conversation. Choose the correct verb forms, nouns, and quantifiers. Then listen to the conversation and check your work.

Pete: Hi, Mom. How are you?

Lulu: So-so. Actually, I'm a little upset.

Pete: Why? What happened?

Lulu: Someone stole my wallet.

Pete: Oh, no. How did it happen?

Lulu: I was riding on the bus when someone took my wallet. It was in my handbag.

Pete: Where were you going?

Lulu: I was returning home from Bertha's house. I had my wallet at Bertha's house. I showed Bertha pictures of all of us. I also had my wallet when I got on the bus. I showed my senior citizen's card to the bus driver. But when I got home, I opened my handbag and my wallet wasn't there.

Pete: Did you have a lot of money?

Lulu: No, not much. I had only a few dollars.

Pete: Was there any identification in your wallet?

Lulu: Yes, there was—my senior citizen's card, my Medicare card, and my credit card.

Pete: Did you cancel your credit card?

Lulu: No, not yet. At first I was too upset to do anything. Later, when I tried to call, I got a busy signal.

Pete: Well, it's very important to keep trying. But don't worry about the wallet or the money. The important thing is that you are okay.

Lulu: I know. You're right. I'm really most upset because I lost those pictures of all of us. But I'll call and cancel my credit card in a few minutes.

Pete: I feel terrible about this. I worry about you a lot. I feel bad we live so far apart.

Lulu: I do, too. But that's life. Please don't worry about me. I'm fine.

Pete: I hope so. I'll call again later this afternoon and see how you are.

Lulu: Okay, Pete. Bye.

Pete: Bye, Mom.

Exercise C.2 (Student Book, page 460)

Pete calls his mother again. Complete their conversation. Choose the correct verb forms, nouns, and quantifiers. Then listen to the conversation and check your work.

Lulu: Hello.

Pete: Hi, Mom. How are you now? Did you call about your credit card?

Lulu: Yes, I took care of everything.

Pete: Good. Do you need anything? Do you have enough food in the house?

Lulu: I don't need anything. James was here a while ago. He brought a few groceries. He got a little meat, a few potatoes, a few onions, a few carrots, and some fruit. Right now I'm preparing a meatloaf, and tonight we're going to have a nice dinner together and forget about my wallet.

Pete: Well, now I'm glad that James is your friend.

Lulu: I'm so happy to hear that. James *is* special. When he was here earlier we had a long talk. We're really very happy together, and we would like to get married. I know there is a big age difference, and I know there may be problems, but we're really a good match.

Pete: You know Mom, a few months ago I was very worried that you were dating James. Now I think it's great. I hope you will be very happy.

Lulu: I do, too.

Pete: I'll call you again tomorrow.

Lulu: I love to speak with you, but I know you're very busy. You don't have to call. Give my love to

Elenore and Doug. I spoke to Carol last week. She sounds very happy. I can't wait to meet Dan.

Pete: He seems very nice. It's really wonderful: My daughter and my mother are getting married.

APPENDIX 20 (page A27)

These are the pronunciation symbols used in this text. Listen to the pronunciation of the key words.

VOWELS	
Symbol	Key Word
i^y	beat
ɪ	bit
e^y	bay
ɛ	bet
æ	bat
ɑ	box, car
ɔ	bought, horse
o^w	bone
ʊ	book
u^w	boot
ʌ	but
ə	banana, sister
aɪ	by
aʊ	bound
ɔɪ	boy
ɚ	burn
ɪər	beer
ɛər	bare
ʊ ər	tour

/t/ means that the /t/ sound is said as a voiced sound (like a quick English /d/).

CONSONANTS	
Symbol	Key Word
p	pan
b	ban
t	tip
d	dip
k	cap
g	gap
tʃ	church
dʒ	judge
f	fan
v	van
θ	thing
ð	then
s	sip
z	zip
ʃ	ship
ʒ	measure
h	hot
m	sum
n	sun
ŋ	sung
w	wet
hw	what
l	lot
r	rot
y	yet

Answer Key to Diagnostic and Final Tests

Note: This answer key generally gives the contracted form. You may wish, where appropriate, to accept the full form.

UNIT 1:

Diagnostic Test

I.

2. He **3.** It **4.** They **5.** she **6.** We (You) **7.** He **8.** they **9.** It **10.** They

II.

2. We're **3.** daughter's **4.** I'm **5.** We're **6.** She's **7.** They're **8.** It's **9.** You're **10.** He's

III.

1. (He's not happy.)
2. They aren't sisters. (They're not sisters.)
3. We aren't from Korea. (We're not from Korea.)
4. It isn't a nickel. (It's not a nickel.)
5. It isn't an apostrophe. (It's not an apostrophe.)

IV.

2. Are you students? (Are we students?)
3. Is it one o'clock?
4. Is she from Thailand?
5. Is it a dollar bill?
6. Is he late?
7. Is it late?

V.

2. P.M. **3.** P.M. **4.** P.M.

VI.

2. 1:45 **3.** 3:30 **4.** 1:10

VII.

2. It's three o'clock.
3. He isn't a businessman. (He's not a businessman.)
4. Are you happy?
5. What time is it?
6. Yes, we are.
7. They aren't students.
8. He isn't a detective.
9. I'm a new teacher.
10. Are they from the United States?

UNIT 1:

Final Test

I.

2. They **3.** They **4.** he **5.** We (You) **6.** It **7.** It **8.** It **9.** She **10.** They

II.

2. I'm **3.** We're **4.** They're **5.** She's **6.** friend's **7.** Carol's **8.** You're **9.** It's **10.** He's

III.

1. (They're not worried.)
2. He isn't a great detective. (He's not a great detective.)
3. I'm not an old student.
4. It isn't late. (It's not late.)
5. It isn't midnight. (It's not midnight.)

IV.

2. Are they in the telephone book?
3. Are you homesick?
4. Are you tired? (Are we tired?)
5. Is she safe?
6. Is it eleven fifty-five?
7. Is he in love?

V.

2. A.M. **3.** P.M. **4.** A.M.

VI.

2. 4:15 **3.** 6:50 **4.** 6:45

VII.

2. What time is it?
3. Pete and Milt aren't worried now.
4. She isn't homesick. (She's not homesick.)
5. Where are you from?
6. I'm from Greece.
7. My name is Lulu. (My name's Lulu.)
8. Are you a teacher?
9. We aren't good friends.
10. We aren't from the Moon. We're from Montana. (We're not from the Moon. We're from Montana.)

UNIT 2:

Diagnostic Test

I.

2.—, — **3.** an **4.**— **5.** a **6.** a, a **7.** a **8.**— **9.**— **10.** an

II.

2. friends **3.** watches **4.** grandchildren **5.** eyes **6.** teachers **7.** boxes **8.** dictionaries **9.** brothers **10.** wives

III.

2. Her **3.** our **4.** Her **5.** His **6.** Their **7.** Its **8.** Your

IV.

2. This **3.** This **4.** these **5.** these **6.** this

V.

VI.
2. Its tail is long.
3. These cookies are delicious.
4. The water fountain is next to the cafeteria.
5. My sister is beautiful. Her hair is long and wavy.
6. The bank is near the library.
7. He's a handsome man.
8. Mr. Jones is an engineer.
9. This is a picture of my aunt. Her name is Ann.
10. These are your seats.

UNIT 2:

Final Test

I.
2. — 3. an 4. — 5. a 6. — 7. a 8. a 9. a 10. an

II.
2. women 3. cities 4. Potatoes 5. sisters 6. eyes 7. boxes 8. children 9. pictures 10. sons

III.
2. Their 3. Our 4. His 5. Our 6. Her 7. Its 8. Your

IV.
2. these 3. this 4. These 5. this 6. this

V.

VI.
2. They're tall boys.
3. This is a grammar test.
4. He's a young father.
5. Your seat is here.
6. We're lucky women.
7. This is a turtle. Its name is Myrtle.
8. My aunt is in Korea. Her husband is in California.
9. He's a new student. His name is Carlos.
10. The lamp is next to the desk.

UNIT 3:

Diagnostic Test

I.
2. Whose last name is Smith?
3. Where is the bathroom?
4. Who is late?
5. Whose initials are C. W.?
6. What is your favorite subject?
7. When is his first class? (What time is his first class?)
8. When is the party?

II.
2. at, at 3. at the 4. in 5. on 6. at 7. in the 8. on, At, at 9. in the, in the

III.
2. brother's son
3. mother's sister
4. friend's first name
5. Yoko's dog
6. Juan's composition
7. girls' locker room

IV.
2. Who's 3. Whose 4. Who's 5. Whose

V.
2. fourteenth 3. eighth 4. third 5. ten 6. two 7. seventh

VI.
2. Yuriko's hat is under the table.
3. Where is your grammar book?
4. His office is on the twenty-third floor.
5. The refrigerator is in the kitchen.
6. His friend's book is at school.
7. She's at work at nine o'clock.
8. My birthday is on January 4th.
9. What time is the graduation?
10. My second class is at noon.

UNIT 3:

Final Test

I.
1. (Who's at work?)
2. Where is Lulu Winston from?
3. When is Labor Day?
4. Whose sweater is gray?
5. What is your nickname?
6. When is his birthday party? (What time is his birthday party?)
7. Whose pen is blue?
8. Where is he?

II.
1. at 2. in the 3. in the 4. at the 5. in the 6. on 7. at 8. on 9. in the, at

III.
2. cousin's roommate
3. friend's grandmother
4. children's bedroom
5. dog's name
6. boys' bathroom

IV.
2. Who's 3. Whose 4. Whose 5. Whose

V.
2. second 3. ten 4. eighth 5. third 6. first 7. Four

VI.
2. My mother's mother is my grandmother.
3. There's a TV in the living room.
4. That program is on TV at night.
5. Her apartment is on the sixth floor.

6. Who's late?
7. November is the eleventh month of the year.
8. Her graduation is in June.
9. The girls' gym is on this floor.
10. Is this Yoko's pen?

UNIT 4:

Diagnostic Test

I.

2. b. Let's have dinner.
3. b. Let's leave.
4. a. Please open the window.
5. a. Hurry.
6. a. Then read them to your partner.
7. a. Please be quiet.

II.

2. her 3. me, him 4. them 5. it 6. it 7. them 8. them 9. us
10. you

III.

2. There are some letters in the mailbox.
3. ✓
4. There's a cockroach under the refrigerator.
5. ✓
6. ✓
7. ✓

IV.

2. They are 3. They are 4. There are 5. There are
6. There are 7. They are

V.

2. a lot of 3. aren't many 4. several 5. aren't any 6. a few

VI.

2. How many 3. Are there 4. Are they 5. Is it 6. How many
7. Is she

VII.

2. and 3. but (and) 4. but (and) 5. and 6. but

VIII.

2. Let's buy a new TV.
3. There are several bookstores on this street.
4. How many teachers are there in your school?
5. Don't ask us.
6. There are a lot of apples in the refrigerator.
7. Don't buy any oranges.
8. There's a picture on the wall.
9. The meeting is important, but only a few people are here.
10. She's good in languages. Ask her your questions.

UNIT 4:

Final Test

I.

2. a. Let's buy a bottle of soda.
3. b. Take an umbrella.
4. a. Please open the door.

5. b. Please don't speak loud.
6. b. Please don't open the oven.
7. a. Please be quiet.

II.

2. them 3. them 4. you 5. her 6. him 7. us 8. it 9. them 10. him

III.

2. There's a napkin under the table.
3. ✓
4. There isn't a cloud in the sky.
5. There's a chicken in the kitchen.
6. ✓
7. There's a mailbox on the corner.

IV.

2. They are 3. There are 4. They are 5. There are 6. They are

V.

2. a lot of 3. several 4. one 5. aren't many 6. a few

VI.

2. How many 3. Are they 4. Is there 5. Is she 6. Is he 7. Is it

VII.

2. and 3. and 4. but 5. and 6. but

VIII.

2. Let's ask them about the party.
3. Please open the window.
4. Help her.
5. There are a lot of bananas in this bag.
6. Are there many students in your class?
7. How many cars are there in the garage?
8. There are lots of flowers in the garden.
9. There are a few good bakeries on this street.
10. Is there a ladies' room on this floor?

UNIT 5:

Diagnostic Test

I.

1. (is crying)
2. 's raining
3. 'm not wearing
4. 'm studying
5. 're not working (aren't working)
6. 's drinking
7. 's standing

II.

1. I'm not.
2. Are Mr. and Mrs. White talking on the telephone right now?
   they are.
3. Is Juan reading a magazine at this time?
   he isn't. (he's not.)
4. Am I sitting in your seat?
   you are.
5. Are you and I doing the right thing?
   we are.

III.

1. He's in Toronto. (In Toronto.)
2. What is Wei Liang doing in Toronto?
   He's studying English.

3. Is it raining in Toronto now?
   No, it isn't. (No, it's not.)
4. What's Wei Liang wearing?
   He's wearing a sweatshirt, wool pants, and boots.
5. Why is Wei Liang wearing a sweatshirt, wool pants, and boots?
   His room is very cold.
6. What's Pedro doing now?
   He's skiing.
7. Where is Pedro skiing?
   In the Laurentian Mountains. (He's skiing in the Laurentian Mountains.)
8. Who's writing a letter?
   Wei Liang. (Wei Liang is.) (Wei Liang is writing a letter.)

IV.

2. We are standing near the bank now.
3. She's wearing two sweaters because it's cold.
4. Who's talking on the phone?
5. Why are they working on Sunday?
6. Is he laughing?
7. Who is sitting next to the window now? (Who's sitting next to the window now?)
8. She's crying because she's lonely.
9. We are eating and drinking.
10. Is it raining in Paris?

UNIT 5:

Final Test

I.

2. 's studying
3. 'm not doing
4. 's taking
5. 'm crying
6. are trying
7. 're not watching (aren't watching)

II.

1. it isn't. ('s not.)
2. Is Dr. Smith seeing patients
   he is. (she is.)
3. Are we landing?
   we are.
4. Are they watching TV?
   they aren't. (they're not.)
5. Is the baby wearing a sweater?
   he is. (she is.)

III.

1. Yes, she is.
2. Is Maria buying toys?
   No, she isn't. (No, she's not.)
3. How many classes is Maria taking?
   Three classes. (She's taking three classes.)
4. What's Maria doing now?
   She's taking a break. (She's taking a break and writing this letter.)
5. Is it raining now?
   Yes, it is.
6. Where is Maria sitting?
   In the back of the store. (Maria is sitting in the back of the store.)
7. What's Maria doing in the back of the store?
   She's sitting and writing a letter. (She's taking a break.)

8. Why is Maria sitting in the back of the store?
   Because it's raining. (Maria is sitting in the back of the store because it's raining.)

IV.

2. Where are you living now?
3. She is watching a movie on TV.
4. He isn't selling his car. (He's not selling his car.)
5. I'm working and studying, too.
6. Why is she standing?
7. Who is listening to the radio now?
8. What is she doing?
9. Is it snowing now?
10. What are you studying?

UNIT 6:

Diagnostic Test

I.

1. takes
2. stays, watches
3. have, don't have
4. don't like, don't have
5. rains, rains
6. doesn't need, has
7. wear, wear
8. works, teaches
9. doesn't snow
10. doesn't go, goes

II.

1. he doesn't
2. Does, cost
   it does
3. Do, speak
   they don't
4. Do, know
   we don't
5. Does, live
   she does
6. Does, visit
   he does
7. Do, have
   I do (we do)
8. Do, know
   don't

III.

2. Are 3. Do 4. Does 5. Is 6. Do 7. Are 8. Is 9. Does 10. Do

IV.

1. Because his old one has a hole in it.
2. do the boys usually study?
   At the library.
3. do we do/do we exchange
   Exchange gifts. (We exchange gifts.)/Gifts.
4. loves to listen to opera?
   My father does.
5. do they eat a big meal?
   In the evening.
6. do you get up?
   At 7:00 A.M.
7. does he wear at his job?
   A suit and tie.

8. do they eat a lot of turkey?
Because it's their favorite food.

V.

2. visits her cousins once a month?
does she visit once a month?
3. helps us with our homework?
does the teacher help?
4. meets his friends in the park?
does he often meet?

VI.

2. That **3.** this **4.** These **5.** This, That, Those

VII.

2. one, ones **3.** one, ones **4.** It **5.** ones

VIII.

2. He doesn't go to school on Saturday.
3. It doesn't rain in the desert.
4. Those are navy, but this one is black.
5. She doesn't live in the city.
6. Does she work in a hospital?
7. When does he arrive?
8. This film is sad. (These films are sad.)
9. What time does the sun rise?
10. Who lives in that house?

UNIT 6:

Final Test

I.

2. is, works
3. isn't from, comes
4. costs, need
5. understands, doesn't speak
6. watch, watch
7. don't eat, 'm
8. play, likes, likes
9. doesn't have, takes
10. meet, go

II.

2. Do, need
I do
3. Do, listen
they don't
4. Does, hurt
it doesn't
5. Do, have
we do
6. Do, have
you don't
7. Do, like
I do
8. Does, speak
she doesn't

III.

2. Are **3.** Does **4.** Is **5.** Is **6.** Is **7.** Do **8.** Does **9.** Do **10.** Are

IV.

2. do we begin class?
At nine o'clock.
3. do they play golf?
On Sunday morning.

4. do they have breakfast?
At 8:30.
5. has a house in the country?
Our uncle does.
6. does he live?
In the small house on the corner.
7. do you (we) do after dinner?
We watch TV.
8. does he wear those pants?
Because they're comfortable.

V.

2. writes his family once a month?
does he write once a month?
3. helps patients with their showers?
does that nurse help with their showers?
4. calls his uncle after five o'clock?
does Ray call after five o'clock?

VI.

2. that **3.** these **4.** this **5.** those

VII.

2. it **3.** ones, ones **4.** It **5.** one, one

VIII.

2. Why does he steal?
3. This book is about grammar.
4. Does it rain a lot in Portland?
5. I live alone.
6. We have a car. It is two years old.
7. Does she teach every day?
8. That store doesn't open before ten o'clock.
9. These women are from Europe.
10. What time does your class begin?

UNIT 7:

Diagnostic Test

I.

1. (He watches two or three hours of television every evening.)
2. I often buy fruit at that market.
3. We rarely eat fish.
4. He always eats muffins with his dinner.
5. Three times a day he takes these pills. (He takes these pills three times a day.)
6. They are usually late.

II.

2. How often do Mary and Joe take a vacation?
3. When do you usually pay your rent?
4. How often does he go to the dentist?
5. Why are we eating at a resturant today?
6. What time do they often eat breakfast?
7. What is she wearing to school today?
8. What do you want now?

III.

1. is, don't see, 's walking, see
2. Do, need, don't think, understand, 's, 're learning
3. is, belongs, is, 's studying
4. are, doing, 'm working, Do, want
5. do, think, like, 's using, 're playing
6. do, do, go, do, stay, sounds

IV.

2. She needs new glasses.
3. We don't like to drink soda. (We don't like drinking soda.)
4. We prefer juice.

V.

2. Hers, his 3. Hers 4. yours 5. Theirs 6. yours, ours

VI.

1. (I like playing golf.)
2. They're working at home.
3. Do you need to go to the library?
4. She prefers to drink coffee.
5. That's my new umbrella.
6. What's your brother's first name?
7. Right now she's playing tennis.
8. He owns a two bedroom apartment.
9. I agree.
10. I don't believe you.

UNIT 7:

Final Test

I.

2. She always wears a red hat.
3. Twice a week they water those plants. (They water those plants twice a week.)
4. Once in a while we drive to the mountains. (We drive to the mountains once in a while.)
5. You rarely help with the housework.
6. It often rains in April.

II.

2. How often does she call you?
3. How often do they write to you?
4. Where do they usually go in the evening?
5. Why is he crying now?
6. Who owns that big house?
7. When does your friend usually take a vacation?
8. Where are Jack and Joanne playing at this moment?

III.

2. 's, doing, 's writing, Does, do
3. Do, know, live, 's (is),'s talking
4. Is, cooking, 's cooking, cooks, cooks, don't cook, eat
5. are, agree, have
6. are fighting, aren't fighting ('re not fighting), 're playing

IV.

1. (They like going to the park.)
2. He needs a new watch.
3. I prefer to stay home today. (I prefer staying home today.)
4. She wants a red carpet.

V.

2. Mine 3. yours, Mine 4. His 5. Ours 6. hers

VI.

2. I always eat a big breakfast.
3. My eyes are blue.
4. She prefers to play tennis. (She prefers playing tennis.)
5. I need a new tennis racket.
6. How often do you paint your apartment?
7. Right now we are polishing the furniture.

8. I agree with you.
9. I want to study physics.
10. He needs to find a new apartment.

UNIT 8:

Diagnostic Test

I.

2. called, didn't visit
3. fell, broke
4. didn't walk, drove
5. baked, finished
6. didn't watch, played
7. met, took, saw
8. drank, left
9. missed, came
10. went, played

II.

2. ago 3. Yesterday 4. Last 5. Yesterday

III.

1. changed, left
2. did, go, played, went
3. did, eat, ate, had
4. Did, read, read
5. Did, bring, brought

IV.

2. helped that older man?
   did your friends help?
3. called her father on Sunday?
   did Maria call on Sunday?

V.

1. don't feel, 'm, caught
2. Did, finish, 'm finishing
3. Do, have, bought, 're driving
4. Is, crying, lost
5. 's playing, plays, joined, 's

VI.

2. Did they bake a cake?
3. She went to San Francisco on vacation two months ago.
4. Two weeks ago we returned that chair.
5. What happened at the party last night?
6. Did it rain during the ball game?
7. We didn't visit the museum.
8. What did you borrow from your friend?

UNIT 8:

Final Test

I.

1. asked
2. didn't find, hid
3. forgot
4. fought, didn't get
5. worked, became
6. borrowed, forgot
7. didn't understand, asked

8. did, wrote, read
9. didn't wear, had
10. left, stole

II.

2. Yesterday **3.** Last **4.** Last **5.** ago

III.

1. finished
2. ate
3. did, lose, didn't lose, stole
4. did, call, told
5. did, buy, didn't buy, gave

IV.

2. met their teacher at the park?
   did the boys meet at the park?
3. saw his mother at the supermarket?
   did Bill see at the supermarket?

V.

1. are, doing, 'm cleaning, hate
2. are, making, made, saw, did
3. Did, rain, 's raining, Do, have, have
4. taught, loved, Did, give, learned
5. play, didn't play
6. Did, play

VI.

2. Did you eat turkey last night?
3. It didn't work.
4. Why did you come late this morning?
5. When did the movie begin?
6. Did we have a test last week?
7. Two weeks ago the men worked on the bridge.
8. Who found the book last night?

UNIT 9:

Diagnostic Test

I.

1. 's **2.** were, 're **3.** 'm, 's **4.** were, 're **5.** 's

II.

2. Was **3.** Are **4.** Do **5.** Does **6.** Were **7.** Is **8.** Did **9.** Were
10. Am

III.

1. Who was late last week?
2. Where did he buy those paintings?
3. When were they in Paris?
4. Why did she wear a long skirt?
5. How were your classes last year?
6. What was your favorite game as a child?
7. What did you do yesterday after school?

IV.

2. Was there **3.** There's **4.** Are there **5.** Were there
6. There aren't **7.** There wasn't **8.** There was

V.

1. bought
2. caught, missed
3. met, went
4. rode
5. began, finished
6. chose
7. didn't kick, threw

8. wrote
9. built
10. didn't understand

VI.

2. Was she at the movies last night?
3. Today we were busy.
4. They were at a party at the International Center.
5. Were there any questions at the end of his speech?
6. Who was late yesterday?
7. When were they in class last week?
8. There wasn't a cup in the kitchen.
9. There weren't any erasers in the classroom.
10. Where were you this morning?

UNIT 9:

Final Test

I.

1. 's **2.** were, 're **3.** 's **4.** were, were, 're **5.** 'm

II.

2. Is **3.** Was **4.** Am **5.** Were **6.** Does **7.** Do **8.** Are **9.** Were **10.** Did

III.

2. Who was with you on your trip last month?
3. What did they see at the museum yesterday?
4. When was he at the library?
5. How was your first day at work?
6. Where did she get those boots?
7. Why were they angry last night?

IV.

2. There's **3.** Is there **4.** Was there **5.** Were there
6. There aren't **7.** There are **8.** There was

V.

1. rode
2. ate, drank
3. came, stayed
4. laughed, cried
5. spent, didn't spend
6. wore, didn't wear
7. brought, had
8. read, discussed
9. wrote
10. didn't know

VI.

2. Were you on time last Monday?
3. When were you at the doctor last year?
4. Last year they were in the third year of high school.
5. What were you afraid of?
6. There weren't any lemons in the refrigerator.
7. Was she the teacher last year, too?
8. Who was here last night?
9. I was at the library from nine to three yesterday.
10. When were there problems?

UNIT 10:

Diagnostic Test

I.

2. some **3.** an **4.** Some **5.** a little **6.** a few **7.** any **8.** any
9. many **10.** One

II.

2. — 3. sweatshirts 4. — 5. bowls 6. — 7. eggs 8. chairs
9. waitresses 10. friends

III.

2. How much 3. How many 4. How much 5. How many
6. How much

IV.

2. pound 3. quart (cup) 4. cup 5. teaspoon 6. tube

V.

2. enough 3. too much 4. too little 5. too many 6. too few

VI.

2. May I help you?
3. I can't understand him.
4. Could I please borrow your pen?
5. Could you please help me carry these boxes?
6. I couldn't understand him.

VII.

2. Where would you like to go?
3. How many people went to the game?
4. There weren't enough students to have a class.
5. She can type sixty words a minute.
6. How many rolls of film did you buy?
7. Did she give us a lot of homework?
8. How many cups of coffee did you drink?
9. What would she like to do after lunch?
10. There are a few problems in your report.

UNIT 10:

Final Test

I.

2. many 3. One 4. a little 5. a few 6. any 7. a 8. some 9. much
10. some

II.

2. — 3. —, —, — 4. chairs 5. —, — 6. shoes 7. —, — 8. —
9. —, — 10. magazines

III.

2. How many 3. How much 4. How much 5. How many
6. How much

IV.

2. gallon 3. pound 4. roll 5. bowl 6. tablespoon

V.

2. too many 3. too many 4. too few 5. too little 6. enough

VI.

2. May I borrow your pen?
3. Can you type?
4. How can I get to the library from here?
5. Yes. I'd like some strawberries and cream, please.
6. I couldn't find mine.

VII.

2. We did our homework together.
3. Could I please see your report?
4. How much juice did they drink?

5. I'd like to visit them next week.
6. She has many relatives in this country.
7. Please don't buy any fruit.
8. She can ski very well.
9. We saw a little snow on the top of the mountain.
10. Several students stayed home last Monday.

UNIT 11:

Diagnostic Test

I.

1. isn't going to go to school. ('s not going to go to school.)
2. 's going to study all day Monday.
   isn't going to study Tuesday night. ('s not going to study Tuesday night.)
3. aren't going to go on a picnic. ('re not going to go on a picnic.) 're going to stay home and watch videos.
4. They aren't going to stay in the city. (They're not going to stay in the city.)
   They're going to buy a house and move to the country.
5. I'm not going to watch that movie.
   I'm going to sleep.

II.

1. worked, 's going to go
2. picked, gave, 's going to bake
3. 's going to come, spoke, told
4. finished, are, going to return
5. lost, 'm going to buy, 'm going to buy

III.

2. 's flying 3. 's taking 4. 's flying 5. 's returning 6. 's paying
7. 'm not paying

IV.

2. I'll help you.
3. I won't be home until 10:00 P.M.
4. I'll be back in five minutes.
5. He won't apologize.

V.

2. might, 'll 3. may 4. won't 5. will, won't

VI.

2. John is writing a letter.
3. John writing a letter
4. John write a letter
5. John going to write a letter (John writing a letter)
6. John write a letter
7. John writing a letter
8. John write a letter

VII.

1. 'm studying, 's, 'm going to take, Are, 'll join
2. was, Did, buy, bought, 'm going to return ('m returning), were
3. does, come, 'm going to check ('m checking), are, waiting, borrowed, told
4. 'll be, Was, was, put
5. is, Are, going to do (doing), 're going to have, ('re having)

VIII.

2. We'll be home tonight.
3. When are we going to see the doctor?
4. How are we going to get there by eleven o'clock?

5. Next year she's going to graduate from college.
6. May I help you?
7. Who is he going to invite?
8. Just ask her and I'm sure she'll help.
9. Next week they're going to take a vacation.
10. Take your umbrella. It might rain.

UNIT 11:

Final Test

I.

1. He's not going to keep his new one in his pocket. (He isn't going to keep his new one in his pocket.)
2. I'm not going to visit my aunt today.
   I'm going to visit my aunt tomorrow.
3. We aren't going to buy a new car. (We're not going to buy a new car.)
   We're going to buy a used car.
4. I'm not going to buy any carrots.
   I'm going to buy some lettuce.
5. She's going to drink a glass of water.
   She's not going to eat anything. (She isn't going to eat anything.)

II.

1. gave, 're going to get
2. looked, didn't find, 's going to look
3. went, heard, enjoyed, 're going to go
4. was, forgot, didn't return, 's going to pay
5. didn't take, 'm going to take

III.

2. 're driving
3. Are, staying
4. 're driving
5. 'm going
6. 're leaving
7. returning

IV.

2. He'll explain it to you.
3. He won't eat it.
4. He won't tell me.
5. I'll help you.

V.

2. 'll, might 3. 'll 4. won't 5. may

VI.

2. Janet is painting a picture.
3. Janet painting a picture
4. Janet paint a picture
5. Janet paint a picture
6. Janet going to paint a picture (Janet painting a picture)
7. Janet didn't paint a picture.
8. Janet isn't going to paint a picture. (Janet's not going to paint a picture.) (Janet isn't painting a picture.) (Janet's not painting a picture.)

VII.

1. went, is, going to get (getting), wants
2. is, going to leave (leaving), is, going to take (taking), are driving (are going to drive), 'll need ('re going to need), Do, think

3. did, do, got, Do, like, 's (is), 'm going ('m going to go)
4. don't know, 's (is), 'll fix
5. are going to get (are getting), won't tell

VIII.

1. Who's going to return the jacket?
2. She might take an art course.
3. When are you going to study biology?
4. Next week there's going to be an art exhibit in the university library.
5. Will you marry me?
6. He won't wear his glasses.
7. How are we getting to school today?
8. It may snow tonight. Don't forget your boots.
9. I'm going to do the laundry.
10. How long are they going to be away?

UNIT 12:

Diagnostic Test

I.

2. A car is more expensive than a bicycle.
3. A mountain is higher than a hill.
4. An ocean is bigger than a river.

II.

2. good 3. slowly 4. softly 5. hard 6. hard 7. fluently 8. careful 9. bad 10. badly

III.

2. Do men eat faster than women?
3. Do men drive more carefully than women?
4. Do doctors work harder than nurses?

IV.

2. very 3. too 4. too

V.

2. from 3. than 4. as 5. as 6. than 7. than 8. from

VI.

2. fewer 3. less 4. fewer 5. more 6. less

VII.

2. a. bigger than
3. c. more expensive
4. a. late
5. b. quickly
6. a. carefully than
7. b. worse
8. b. old enough
9. a. as important as

VIII.

2. He's strong enough to be a weight lifter.
3. An elephant is bigger than a dog.
4. She writes well.
5. My sister is very different from my brother.
6. Are you as old as your cousin?
7. There were fewer people than last year.
8. This is a more comfortable chair than the other chair.
9. That's a very nice tie.
10. She has a busier schedule than he does.

UNIT 12:

Final Test

I.

2. A rabbit is faster than a turtle.
3. A diamond is more expensive than a pearl.
4. A fur jacket is warmer than a jeans jacket.

II.

2. slowly **3.** openly **4.** late **5.** carefully **6.** clever **7.** bad
8. friendly **9.** quickly **10.** accurate

III.

2. Do men drive more slowly than women?
3. Do lions run faster than tigers?
4. Does fried chicken taste better than broiled chicken?

IV.

2. too **3.** very **4.** too

V.

2. from **3.** than **4.** than **5.** as **6.** as **7.** than **8.** than

VI.

2. fewer **3.** less **4.** fewer **5.** more **6.** less

VII.

2. a. accurately
3. c. bad as
4. a. heavier than
5. b. faster than
6. a. big enough
7. a. more generous than
8. c. better

VIII.

2. There's less homework today so we have time to study for the test.
3. Are you experienced enough to be the director?
4. Does he work as quickly as his partner does?
5. Is it as late as I think?
6. Is the bracelet more expensive than the earrings?
7. He works harder than his boss does.
8. She sings very well.
9. That's a very beautiful vest.
10. Today's news is worse than yesterday's news.

UNIT 13:

Diagnostic Test

I.

2. rang, was taking
3. was skiing, fell, broke
4. were sleeping, flew
5. Were, shaving, cut
6. rang, ran, answered

II.

2. for **3.** for, to **4.** to **5.** to **6.** for

III.

2. They gave it to that hospital.

3. She read them to the children.
4. We built it for our dog.
5. I showed them to my friends.
6. He told it to the judge.

IV.

2. are, too
3. didn't, either
4. can't, either
5. isn't, either
6. won't, either
7. would, too

V.

2. off **3.** in **4.** back **5.** off

VI.

2. broke down **3.** catches on **4.** clear up **5.** grew up

VII.

2. I didn't do my homework and my friend didn't, either.
3. We were driving across the bridge when our car broke down.
4. Would you explain that sentence to me?
5. She sent me a box of cookies.
6. We were listening to the radio when we heard about that accident.
7. Please don't leave your clothes on the chair. Hang them up.
8. Would you please throw them away.
9. Give it to me.
10. Why were you standing in the rain?

UNIT 13:

Final Test

I.

1. saw
2. came, were baking
3. was playing, got
4. was shaving
5. were driving, heard
6. ate, drove

II.

2. to **3.** for **4.** for **5.** for **6.** for

III.

2. She showed them to us.
3. We bought it for our son.
4. They told it to their parents.
5. He made it for me.
6. I owe it to the bank.

IV.

2. does, too
3. are, too
4. 'm not, either
5. weren't, either
6. can, too
7. didn't, either

V.

2. up **3.** on **4.** away **5.** up

VI.

2. hung up 3. stood up 4. break down 5. come up

VII.

2. He doesn't speak Turkish and his wife doesn't, either.
3. He can't explain that joke to me.
4. Who was standing on the roof?
5. He's a good cook, but he doesn't like to cook. He prefers to eat out.
6. I found a good carpenter for you.
7. He gave it to him.
8. What were you doing last night at eleven o'clock?
9. I was talking on the telephone when the doorbell rang.
10. I like fish and he does, too.

UNIT 14:

Diagnostic Test

I.

2. shouldn't 3. should, shouldn't 4. should

II.

2. 'd better not
3. 'd better
4. 'd better

III.

2. don't have to
3. has to (must)
4. doesn't have to
5. has to

IV.

2. has to 3. had to 4. had to 5. have to

V.

2. can
3. 'd better not
4. Would
5. ought
6. don't have to

VI.

2. the longest
3. the highest
4. the biggest
5. the most expensive
6. the most dangerous
7. the earliest
8. the busiest

VII.

2. the best
3. worse than
4. more important than
5. the friendliest
6. more generous than
7. warmer than
8. the most handsome

VIII.

2. She'd better walk to work.
3. It isn't safe to stand in the rowboat. You mustn't stand in it. (You shouldn't stand in it.)

4. What should we take to the beach?
5. Last week we had to work until 10:00 P.M.
6. He is one of the most industrious workers in the company.
7. He ought to get new front tires.
8. Next week she has to go to the dentist.
9. You'd better not leave your ring in the bathroom.
10. Who is the most experienced secretary of the three?

UNIT 14:

Final Test

I.

2. shouldn't 3. shouldn't 4. should

II.

2. 'd better not
3 'd better not
4. 'd better

III.

2. has to
3. mustn't
4. doesn't have to
5. don't have to

IV.

2. have to 3. had to 4. has to 5. had to

V.

2. might, might
3. ought
4. don't have to
5. mustn't
6. shouldn't

VI.

2. the most accurately
3. the most beautiful
4. the smallest
5. the funniest
6. the fastest
7. the most important
8. the cheapest

VII.

2. the hardest
3. the best
4. more comfortable than
5. the coldest
6. colder than
7. earlier than
8. the fastest

VIII.

2. He is the tallest one in the class.
3. They shouldn't complain so much.
4. Last month I had to take three important tests.
5. She ought to spend less money.
6. That is one of the most important discoveries of the century.
7. That pot is very hot. You mustn't touch it.
8. Does she have to work all summer?
9. Thanksgiving is one of the most important holidays of the year.
10. I want her to drive. She drives the most carefully of all.

Diagnostic and Final Tests

These exams test the material presented in the grammar charts, grammar notes, and Focused Practice exercises. The results of each Diagnostic Test enable you to tailor your class to the needs of individual students. The format of both the Diagnostic and Final Tests is the same, and all but the final section of each test are labeled by grammar point. This labeling allows you to pinpoint each student's particular strengths and weaknesses within the unit. Students can concentrate on the sections in which they are weakest. They can work alone at their own pace or with others who need to practice the same areas. The final section of each test is called Synthesis: Error Correction and covers the grammar points of the entire unit. The errors shown reflect the most common mistakes students make. As students correct these errors, they begin to correct their own.

Students who do well on the unit's Diagnostic Test should feel good about their high scores, but they should also realize that knowledge of a language requires communication in open-ended situations. If these students are weak in comprehension or communication skills, they should concentrate on the Listening and Communication Practice exercises in the book.

Students who do poorly on the Diagnostic Test will want to divide their time between the Focused Practice and Communication Practice exercises.

Heterogeneous classes (beginners, false beginners, and students at a higher level) can be divided into groups that concentrate on the kinds of exercises they need the most. The teacher can work with the different groups and help each student to overcome his or her weaknesses.

The Final Test for each unit gives students the chance to make certain they understand the grammar points presented in the unit. The tests are straightforward, and since the format is the same part by part as on the Diagnostic Test, the Final Test offers students who have studied the chance to succeed and gain a sense of accomplishment and confidence in their ability to learn and understand grammar.

Unit 1: Diagnostic Test

I. Subject Pronouns

Change the underlined words to **I, you, he, she, it, we**, *or* **they**. *Use capital letters where necessary.*

1. <u>The businessmen</u> are in the restaurant. *They are in the restaurant.* _____

2. <u>Pete Winston</u> is a father. _____

3. <u>Oregon State University</u> is big, clean, and beautiful. _____

4. <u>The people</u> are friendly. _____

5. Is <u>my sister</u> worried? _____

6. <u>You and your brother</u> are new students. _____

7. <u>My boyfriend</u> isn't a detective. _____

8. Are <u>the girls</u> roommates? _____

9. <u>The university</u> is in Washington, D.C. _____

10. <u>The men</u> are worried. _____

II. Contractions with *Be*

Change the underlined words to contractions.

1. <u>It is</u> clean here. *It's clean here.* _____

2. <u>We are</u> old friends. _____

3. His <u>daughter is</u> in love. _____

4. <u>I am</u> in a college town. _____

5. <u>We are</u> roommates. _____

6. <u>She is</u> from France. _____

7. <u>They are</u> late. _____

8. <u>It is</u> in Asia. _____

9. <u>You are</u> a teacher. _____

10. <u>He is</u> happy. _____

III. Negative Statements with *Be*

Change each sentence in parentheses to the negative. Write it below. Use contractions.

1. (He's happy.)

   _____He isn't happy._____ He's worried.

2. (They are sisters.)

   _____ They are roommates.

3. (We are from Korea.)

   _____ We are from China.

4. (It's a nickel.)

   _____ It's a quarter.

5. (It's an apostrophe.)

   _____ It's a comma.

IV. *Yes/No* Questions with *Be*

Read the answers. Write questions. Use the words in parentheses.

1. A: _____Are you a detective?_____ (a detective)

   B: No, I'm not. I'm a businessman.

2. A: _____ (students)

   B: No, we aren't. We're teachers.

3. A: _____ (one o'clock)

   B: Yes. It's just one o'clock.

4. A: _____ (from Thailand)

   B: No, she's not. She's from China.

5. A: _____ (a dollar bill)

   B: No, it's a ten-dollar bill.

6. A: _____ (late)

   B: Yes, he is.

7. A: _____ (late)

   B: No, it's not. It's early.

V. *It's* + Time: A.M. and P.M.

Add A.M. or P.M. after the time.

1. It's midnight. It's 12:00 <u>A.M.</u> .

2. It's noon. It's 12:00 ———— .

3. It's three o'clock in the afternoon. It's 3:00 ———— .

4. It's eight o'clock in the evening. It's 8:00 ———— .

VI. Telling Time: Numbers

Write the time in numbers.

1. Eight thirty-five <u>8:35</u>

2. A quarter to two ————

3. Three-thirty ————

4. Ten after one ————

VII. Synthesis: Error Correction

Correct these sentences.

1. It's one-thirty o'clock. <u>It's one-thirty.</u>

2. It's three o'clocks. ————————

3. He is no a businessman. ————————

4. You happy? ————————

5. What time it is? ————————

6. Yes, we're. ————————

7. They isn't students. ————————

8. He isn't no a detective. ————————

9. I,m a new teacher. ————————

10. Are they from the United States. ————————

Unit 1: Final Test

I. Subject Pronouns

Change the underlined words to **I, you, he, she, it, we**, *or* **they**. *Use capital letters where necessary.*

     She
1. ~~My daughter~~ is in love.
2. The detectives are friends.
3. The telephones are old.
4. Is your father in Canada?
5. You and your classmate are on time.
6. Michigan is near Wisconsin.
7. The telephone book is big.
8. Is English easy for you?
9. Aunt Abby is in Wisconsin.
10. The girls are busy.

II. Contractions with *Be*

Change the underlined words to contractions.

    It's
1. It is in Corvallis.
2. I am worried about you.
3. We are from Canada.
4. They are from the United States.
5. She is a new teacher.
6. My friend is a plumber.
7. Carol is a student at Oregon State University.
8. You are wrong.
9. It is late.
10. He is friendly.

III. Negative Statements with *Be*

Change the sentence in parentheses to the negative. Write it below. Use contractions.

1. (They're worried.)

    They aren't worried.   They're happy.
_____

2. (He's a great detective.)

_____ He's not careful.

3. (I'm an old student.)

_____ This is my first course.

4. (It's late.)

_____ It's only six o'clock.

5. (It's midnight.)

_____ It's eleven o'clock.

IV. _Yes/No_ Questions with _Be_

Read the answers. Write questions. Use the words in parentheses.

1. A: _____Is he your roommate?_____ (your roommate)

   B: No, he's not. He's my brother.

2. A: _____ (in the telephone book)

   B: No, they aren't.

3. A: _____ (homesick)

   B: No, I'm not. I'm happy and comfortable in this city.

4. A: _____ (tired)

   B: No, we're not.

5. A: _____ (safe)

   B: Yes, she is. She's safe with Rocky.

6. A: _____ (eleven fifty-five)

   B: No. It's eleven o'clock.

7. A: _____ (in love)

   B: Yes, he is.

V. _It's_ + Time: A.M. and P.M.

Add A.M. or P.M. after the time.

1. I'm hungry. Let's have lunch. It's 1:00 __P.M.__

2. I'm tired. It's already midnight. It's 12:00 _____.

3. The dinner party is at 8:00 _____.

4. It's early in the morning. It's 5:00 _____.

VI. Telling Time: Numbers

Write the time in numbers.

1. Two-fifteen 2:15

2. A quarter past four ———

3. Ten to seven ———

4. Six forty-five ———

VIII. Synthesis: Error Correction

Correct these sentences.

1. Is he a student. Is he a student? _____

2. What time it's? _____

3. Pete and Milt isn't worried now. _____

4. She no is homesick. _____

5. Where you from? _____

6. I from Greece. _____

7. My name be Lulu. _____

8. You a teacher? _____

9. We aren,t good friends. _____

10. We no are from the Moon. We're from Montana. _____

Unit 2: Diagnostic Test

I. Articles: *A, An*

Complete the sentences. Use **a**, **an**, *or leave the line blank.*

1. This is ___a___ quarter. It's not ___a___ nickel.

2. We are _____ teachers. We are not _____ students.

3. He's _____ engineer.

4. They're _____ businesswomen.

5. This is _____ delicious apple.

6. This is _____ hospital. It's not _____ hotel.

7. Is your mother-in-law _____ detective?

8. Is your mother-in-law _____ friendly?

9. Are they _____ roommates?

10. My class is _____ hour long.

II. Plurals of Count Nouns

Complete the sentences. Use the plural form of the nouns in parentheses.

1. My ___children___ are in school.
   (child)

2. Our _____ are in Turkey.
   (friend)

3. These _____ are from Switzerland.
   (watch)

4. They are my _____ .
   (grandchild)

5. Her _____ are blue.
   (eye)

6. Are your _____ from Canada?
   (teacher)

7. The _____ are open.
   (box)

8. The _____ are heavy.
   (dictionary)

9. His _____ are in Korea.
   (brother)

10. Our _____ are early.
    (wife)

III. Possessive Adjectives

Complete the sentences. Use **my, your, his, her, its, their,** *or* **our.** *Use capital letters where necessary.*

1. I am a new student. _____My_____ name is Yoko Mori.

2. She is from France. _____ home is in Paris.

3. We're late. It's 9:15 and _____ class is at 9:00.

4. Lucille is my aunt's real name. _____ nickname is Lulu.

5. My father-in-law is a businessman. _____ office is on 42nd Street.

6. All the Kramers are away. Dr. and Mrs. Kramer are in Australia. _____ children are in Italy.

7. That book is old. _____ cover is torn.

8. You are lucky. _____ classmates are helpful and friendly.

IV. Demonstrative Pronouns: *This/These*

Complete the conversations. Use **this** *or* **these.** *Use capital letters where necessary.*

1. A: What's _____this_____?

   B: It's a cockroach.

2. A: What's expensive?

   B: _____ blouse is expensive.

3. A: Whose problem is it?

   B: _____ is my problem.

4. A: What are _____?

   B: They're donuts. They're delicious.

5. A: Are _____ towels dirty?

   B: Yes, they are.

6. A: Is _____ sweater from Italy?

   B: Yes, it is. It's my favorite sweater.

V. Prepositions of Place

Do the following:

1. Draw a desk.

2. Draw a lamp on the desk.

3. Draw a blackboard behind the desk.

4. Draw a bookcase near the desk.

5. Draw a wastepaper basket between the desk and the bookcase.

6. Draw a dog under the desk.

VI. Synthesis: Error Correction

Correct these sentences.

1. It's a desk heavy. _It's a heavy desk._ _____

2. It's tail is long. _____

3. These cookie are delicious. _____

4. The water fountain is next the cafeteria. _____

5. My sister is beautiful. His hair is long and wavy. _____

6. The bank is near to the library. _____

7. He's handsome man. _____

8. Mr. Jones is a engineer. _____

9. This is a picture of my aunt. She name is Ann. _____

10. These are you seats. _____

Unit 2: Final Test

I. Articles: *A, An*

*Complete the sentences. Use **a, an**, or leave the line blank.*

1. He's __a__ new student.

2. We're ——— actors.

3. He's ——— engineer.

4. They are ——— businessmen.

5. She's ——— beautiful woman.

6. These are ——— sharp knives.

7. They're in ——— hotel near the beach.

8. Lulu is ——— grandmother.

9. Vancouver is ——— city in Canada.

10. They're ——— hour late.

II. Plurals of Count Nouns

Complete the sentences. Use the plural form of the nouns in parentheses.

1. Our __teachers__ are young.
   (teacher)

2. These _____ are soldiers.
   (woman)

3. These _____ are safe.
   (city)

4. _____ from Idaho are big and delicious.
   (Potato)

5. My two _____ are tall and thin.
   (sister)

6. Her _____ are blue.
   (eye)

7. These _____ are empty.
   (box)

8. Our _____ are married.
   (child)

9. These are new _____ .
   (picture)

10. Their _____ are plumbers.
    (son)

III. Possessive Adjectives

Complete the sentences. Use **my, your, his, her, its, their,** *or* **our**. *Use capital letters where necessary.*

1. She is a teacher. _____Her_____ students are from all over the world.

2. They are worried. _____ son is sick.

3. We're lucky. _____ business is good.

4. This is my brother. _____ name is Carlos.

5. We're roommates. _____ apartment is in this building.

6. She is a professor. _____ subject is Spanish Literature.

7. This is our grammar book. _____ title is *Focus on Grammar*.

8. You have a room with a bath. _____ room is on the second floor.

IV. Demonstrative Pronouns: *This/These*

Complete the conversations. Use **this** *or* **these**. *Use capital letters where necessary.*

1. A: Hi, John. _____This_____ is my wife, Mary.

   B: Hello, Mary. Nice to meet you.

2. A: What are _____?

   B: They're cupcakes. Try one.

3. A: Is _____ a new picture?

   B: Yes, it is.

4. A: _____ books are heavy.

   B: You're right. They're very heavy.

5. A: Is _____ a chocolate cake?

   B: No, it's a honey cake.

6. A: What's _____?

   B: It's a turtle.

V. Prepositions of Place

Do the following:

1. Draw a tree.

2. Draw a dog under the tree.

3. Draw apples in the tree.

4. Draw a house behind the tree.

5. Draw a man near the tree.

6. Draw a child between the man and the tree.

VI. Synthesis: Error Correction

Correct these sentences.

1. She's strong athlete. _She's a strong athlete._ _____

2. They're talls boys. _____

3. These is a grammar test. _____

4. He's a father young. _____

5. You seat is here. _____

6. We're women lucky. _____

7. This is turtle. It's name is Myrtle. _____

8. My aunt is in Korea. His husband is in California. _____

9. He's a new student. He name is Carlos. _____

10. The lamp is next the desk. _____

Unit 3: Diagnostic Test

I. *Wh-* Questions with *Be: Who, What, Where, Whose, When, What* + Noun

Read the answers. Write the questions that the underlined word or words answer. Use **Who, What, Where, Whose, When, What** + *Noun.*

1. Where are his children? _____

   His children are <u>in the park</u>.

2. _____

   <u>John's</u> last name is Smith.

3. _____

   The bathroom is <u>next to the bedroom</u>.

4. _____

   <u>John</u> is late.

5. _____

   <u>Carol Winston's</u> initials are C. W.

6. _____

   My favorite subject is <u>history</u>.

7. _____

   His first class is <u>at eleven o'clock</u>.

8. _____

   The party is <u>on Monday</u>.

II. Prepositions of Place and Time

Complete the conversations. Use **at, at the, in, in the,** *or* **on**.

1. A: Where's the blue towel?

   B: It's ___in the___ bathroom.

2. A: Is Pete _____ home?

   B: No, he's _____ work.

3. A: Where are the boys?

   B: They're ──────── ball game.

4. A: Is grandpa in the shower?

   B: No, he's ──────── bed.

5. A: When is your graduation?

   B: It's ──────── June 19th.

6. A: What time is the party?

   B: It's ──────── 7:30.

7. A: Are the children in school ──────── morning?

   B: I don't know.

8. A: When is the news ──────── TV?

   B: ──────── 7:30 ──────── night.

9. A: How's the weather?

   B: It's cool ──────── morning and warm ──────── afternoon.

III. Possessive Nouns

Complete each sentence with the possessive form. Use the nouns in parentheses.

1. My ___mother's mother___ is my grandmother.
   (mother, mother)

2. My _____ is my nephew.
   (brother, son)

3. My _____ is my aunt.
   (mother, sister)

4. His _____ is Hiro.
   (friend, first name)

5. Rocky is _____.
   (Yoko, dog)

6. This is _____.
   (Juan, composition)

7. The _____ is on the second floor.
   (girls, locker room)

IV. Questions with *Who* and *Whose*

*Complete the conversations. Use **who's** or **whose**.*

1. A: ___Whose___ book is on the floor?

    B: Bill's book.

2. A: _____ the new teacher?

    B: Lisa Campbell.

3. A: _____ father is an engineer?

    B: Mary's father is.

4. A: _____ in the first row?

    B: My sister and her girlfriend are.

5. A: _____ test is on the floor?

    B: I don't know.

V. Cardinal and Ordinal Numbers

Choose the correct word in parentheses to complete each sentence.

1. This is my ___second___ day at work.
    (two, second)

2. Valentine's Day is on February _____.
    (fourteen, fourteenth)

3. Our seats are in the _____ row.
    (eight, eighth)

4. This is our _____ holiday this semester.
    (three, third)

5. She's _____ years old.
    (ten, tenth)

6. We are _____ days late.
    (two, second)

7. What's the _____ letter of the alphabet?
    (seven, seventh)

VI. Synthesis: Error Correction

Correct the sentences.

1. Who's jacket is on the floor? ___Whose jacket is on the floor?___

2. Yuriko hat is under the table. _____

3. Where your grammar book? _____

4. His office is on the twenty-three floor. _____

5. The refrigerator is in kitchen. _____

6. His friend book's is in school. _____

7. She's in work at nine o'clock. _____

8. My birthday is in January 4th. _____

9. What time the graduation is? _____

10. My two class is at noon. _____

Unit 3: Final Test

I. *Wh-* Questions with *Be: Who, What, Where, Whose, When, What* + Noun

Read the answers. Write the questions that the underlined word or words answer. Use **Who, What, Where, Whose, When, What** + *Noun.*

1. Who is at work? _____

    Mr. Green is at work.

2. _____

    Lulu Winston is from <u>Vancouver</u>.

3. _____

    Labor Day is <u>on the first Monday in September</u>.

4. _____

    <u>Bob's</u> sweater is gray.

5. _____

    My nickname is <u>Dee</u>.

6. _____

    His birthday party is <u>at 6 o'clock</u>.

7. _____

    <u>My friend's</u> pen is blue.

8. _____

    He's <u>at the movies</u>.

II. Prepositions of Place and Time

Complete the conversations. Use **at, at the, in, in the**, *or* **on**.

1. A: Is Doug ____in____ school?

    B: No, he's _____ home.

2. A: Where is the iron?

    B: It's _____ kitchen on top of the dishwasher.

3. A: Where are the boys?

    B: They're _____ living room.

4. A: Is Sue there?

   B: No, she's _____ movies.

5. A: Who's _____ dining room?

   B: I don't know.

6. A: What's _____ TV?

   B: Nothing good.

7. A: Is the play _____ 8:00?

   B: No, it's at 7:30.

8. A: Where is the hospital?

   B: It's _____ Main Street next to the post office.

9. A: It's hot now.

   B: You're right, but it's always cool _____ evening and it's cold _____ night.

III. Possessive Nouns

Complete each sentence with the possessive form. Use the nouns in parentheses.

1. My ____sister's friend____ is from Bogota, Colombia.
   (sister, friend)

2. My _____ is good at soccer.
   (cousin, roommate)

3. My _____ is ninety-nine years old.
   (friend, grandmother)

4. Our _____ is next to our bedroom.
   (children, bedroom)

5. Our _____ is Spot.
   (dog, name)

6. The _____ is on the second floor.
   (boys, bathroom)

IV. Questions with *Who* and *Whose*

*Complete the conversation. Use **Who's** or **Whose**.*

1. A: ____Who's____ at the door?

   B: It's Grandma.

2. A: _____ in the bathroom?

   B: No one. It's empty.

3. A: _____ gloves are these?

   B: They're John's.

4. A: _____ watch is this?

   B: I don't know. It's not my watch.

5. A: _____ notebook is under my desk?

   B: Oh, I think it's Joan's notebook.

V. Cardinal and Ordinal Numbers

Choose the correct word in parentheses to complete each sentence.

1. Her father is _____ thirty-five _____ years old.
   (thirty-five, thirty-fifth)

2. I am the _____ son in my family.
   (two, second)

3. There are _____ eggs in the refrigerator.
   (ten, tenth)

4. Our classroom is on the _____ floor.
   (eight, eighth)

5. We are in the _____ row.
   (three, third)

6. The _____ show is at 1:00.
   (one, first)

7. _____ students are absent today.
   (Four, Fourth)

VI. Synthesis: Error Correction

Correct these sentences.

1. Who's lunch is this? _Whose lunch is this?_____

2. My mother mother is my grandmother. _____

3. There a TV in the living room. _____

4. That program is on TV in the night. _____

5. Her apartment is on the six floor. _____

6. Whose late? _____

7. November is the eleven month of the year. _____

8. Her graduation is on June. _____

9. The girls gym is on this floor. _____

10. Is this Yoko pen? _____

Unit 4: Diagnostic Test

I. Imperatives

Write the sentence that matches the situation.

1. The light is red. _Stop._ _____
   - a. Stop.
   - b. Don't stop.

2. I'm hungry. _____
   - a. Let's not have dinner.
   - b. Let's have dinner.

3. This movie is terrible. _____
   - a. Let's not leave.
   - b. Let's leave.

4. It's very warm in here. _____
   - a. Please open the window.
   - b. Please don't open the window.

5. _____ It's late.
   - a. Hurry.
   - b. Don't hurry.

6. Work with a partner. Write three sentences. _____
   - a. Then read them to your partner.
   - b. Then don't read them to your partner.

7. You're in a hospital. _____
   - a. Please be quiet.
   - b. Please don't be quiet.

II. Object Pronouns

Complete the sentences. Use **me, him, her, it, you, us**, *or* **them**.

1. Underline the adjectives. Then read ____them____ to the class.

2. She's very good at math. Ask _____ for help with that math problem.

3. Don't tell _____ your problem. I'm not your boss. Tell _____. He's your boss.

4. There are some oranges and apples in the refrigerator. Let's eat _____ now.

5. I love your poem. Please read _____ to me again.

6. Here's the ice cream. Please put _____ in the refrigerator.

7. Here are the new books. Put _____ on the top shelf.

8. They're traffic officers. Ask _____ for directions.

9. We're lawyers. Ask _____ for help.

10. Go to him. He loves _____ .

III. Word Order of Sentences with *There is/There are*

Put a check (✓) next to the sentences that are correct. Change the sentences that are wrong.

1. There's a shelf on the top dictionary. There's a dictionary on the top shelf. _____

2. There are some mailbox in the letters. _____

3. There are five eggs in the refrigerator. _____

4. There's a refrigerator under the cockroach. _____

5. There isn't a cloud in the sky. _____

6. There are beautiful flowers in the garden. _____

7. There's a bird in the tree. _____

IV. Contrast: *There are/They are*

Complete the sentences. Use **There are** *or* **They are**.

1. ____There are____ six women over there.

2. _____ from Russia.

3. _____ doctors.

4. _____ some new students in our class.

5. _____ two new students from Turkey.

6. _____ a lot of students from Korea.

7. _____ polite and friendly.

V. Quantifiers: *One, A few, Some, Several, Many, A lot of*

Look at the information in the chart. Choose the correct word or words in parentheses.

Class Size: 25 Students

1 from Senegal
3 from Venezuela
5 from Japan
10 from Korea
3 from Poland
1 from Egypt
2 from China

1. There is _____ student from Egypt.
   (one, an)

2. There are _____ students from Korea.
   (a lot, a lot of)

3. There _____ students from China.
   (aren't many, aren't any)

4. There are _____ students from Venezuela.
   (several, a lot of)

5. There _____ students from Greece.
   (aren't any, aren't many)

6. There are _____ students from Poland.
   (a few, a lot of)

VI. Questions: *Is there, Is it, Is she, Is he, Are there, Are they,* and *How many*

Read the answers. Complete the questions.

1. A: ___Is there___ a bookstore on 32nd Street?

   B: Yes, there is.

2. A: _____ students are there in your class?

   B: Twenty-five.

3. A: _____ any pizza places near your school?

   B: No, there aren't.

4. A: _____ from Canada?

   B: No. They're from the United States.

5. A: _____ cold today?

    B: No, it isn't.

6. A: _____ people are absent?

    B: Everyone is here.

7. A: _____ a new teacher?

    B: No, she's an old teacher.

VII. *And* and *But*

Complete the sentences. Use **and** *or* **but**.

1. He is six feet, ___*and*___ his son is also six feet.

2. The weather is warm _____ sunny.

3. The weather is warm, _____ it is humid.

4. He is tall, _____ his three brothers are short.

5. This music is soft _____ romantic.

6. This music is beautiful, _____ it isn't good for dancing.

VIII. Synthesis: Error Correction

1. Please you open the window. It's hot in here. _Please open the window. It's hot in here._

2. Let's to buy a new TV. _____

3. They are several bookstores on this street. _____

4. How many teacher are there in your school? _____

5. Don't ask we. _____

6. There are a lot of apple in the refrigerator. _____

7. Don't to buy any oranges. _____

8. There's a wall on the picture. _____

9. The meeting is important, and only a few people are here. _____

10. She's good in languages. Ask she your questions. _____

Unit 4: Final Test

I. Imperatives

Write the sentence that matches the situation.

1. Shh. The baby is asleep. <u>Please don't wake him.</u>
   - a. Please don't wake him.
   - b. Please wake him.

2. I'm thirsty. _____
   - a. Let's buy a bottle of soda.
   - b. Let's not buy a bottle of soda.

3. It's cloudy. _____
   - a. Don't take an umbrella.
   - b. Take an umbrella.

4. My hands are full. _____
   - a. Please open the door.
   - b. Please don't open the door.

5. This is a hospital. _____
   - a. Please speak loud.
   - b. Please don't speak loud.

6. _____ The cake is not ready.
   - a. Please open the oven.
   - b. Please don't open the oven.

7. This is a library. _____
   - a. Please be quiet.
   - b. Please don't be quiet.

II. Object Pronouns

*Complete the sentences. Use **me, him, her, it, you, us,** or **them.***

1. I'm lost. Please help ____<u>me</u>____ .

2. Read these words. Then study _____ .

3. These are my plants. Please water _____ twice a week.

4. Marry him. He loves _____ very much.

5. She's a doctor. Ask _____ about your back problems.

6. He's the teacher. Ask _____ about the homework.

7. We're worried. Please help _____ .

8. This is my dictionary. I need _____ for this test.

9. Write these sentences. Then read _____ to your partner.

10. He's lost. Show _____ the exit.

III. Word Order of Sentences with *There is/There are*

Put a check (✓) next to the sentences that are correct. Change the sentences that are wrong.

1. There's a computer on the desk. ✓ _____

2. There's a table under the napkin. _____

3. There are several pizza places on Main Street. _____

4. There isn't a sky in the cloud. _____

5. There's a kitchen in the chicken. _____

6. There are some cookies in the jar. _____

7. There's a corner on the mailbox. _____

IV. Contrast: *There are/They are*

Complete the sentences. Use **There are** *or* **They are.**

1. This is a picture of my family. _____There are_____ seven people in it.

2. This is Mr. and Mrs. Green. _____ my neighbors.

3. Please do this letter again. _____ several mistakes in it.

4. These actors are popular. _____ generous and thoughtful, too.

5. _____ no newspapers at this store.

6. John and Mary are doctors. _____ at this hospital now.

V. Quantifiers: *One, A few, Some, Any, Several, Many, A lot of*

Look at the information in the chart. Choose the correct word or words in parentheses to complete the sentences.

> Classroom Items
>
> 1 blackboard
> 3 erasers
> 3 windows
> 2 dictionaries
> 30 chairs

1. There ___aren't any___ radios in the classroom.
   (aren't any, aren't many)
2. There are _____ chairs in the classroom.
   (a lot, a lot of)
3. There are _____ erasers in the classroom.
   (several, a lot of)
4. There is _____ blackboard in the classroom.
   (one, some)
5. There _____ dictionaries in the classroom.
   (aren't any, aren't many)
6. There are _____ windows in the classroom.
   (a few, a lot of)

VI. Questions: *Is there, Is it, Is she, Is he, Are there, Are they,* and *How many*

Read the answers. Complete the questions.

1. A: ___Are there___ many coffee shops on this street?

   B: Yes, there are.

2. A: _____ calories are there in an egg?

   B: I don't know.

3. A: _____ under the table?

   B: No, they're in the closet.

4. A: _____ a lemon in the refrigerator?

   B: No, there isn't.

5. A: _____ the doctor?

   B: Yes, she is.

6. A: _____ your cousin?

   B: No, he's my friend.

7. A: _____ late?

   B: No, it's early.

VII. *And* and *But*

Complete the sentences. Use **and** *or* **but***.*

1. This sweater is beautiful, ___but___ it isn't comfortable.

2. This sweater is beautiful, _____ it isn't expensive.

3. Pizza is delicious, —————— our children love it.

4. This pizza is delicious, —————— it's cold.

5. The horse is strong —————— healthy.

6. The horse is healthy, —————— it is very old.

VIII. **Synthesis: Error Correction**

Correct these sentences.

1. Let's to go to the park. _Let's go to the park._ _____

2. Let's ask they about the party. _____

3. Please you open the window. _____

4. Help she. _____

5. There's a lot of bananas in this bag. _____

6. Are they many students in your class? _____

7. How many car are there in the garage? _____

8. They are lots of flowers in the garden. _____

9. There's a few good bakeries on this street. _____

10. Are there a ladies' room on this floor? _____

Unit 5: Diagnostic Test

I. Present Progressive: Affirmative and Negative Statements

Complete the sentences. Use the affirmative or negative of the present progressive. Use the verbs in the box.

cry	rain	study	work
drink	stand	wear	

1. The baby ____'s crying____ . Please pick him up.

2. Take your umbrella. It _____ .

3. I don't know the time. I _____ my watch.

4. Please don't play that loud music. I _____ for an important test.

5. We _____ because today is a holiday.

6. Al's very thirsty. He _____ all the juice.

7. She _____ because there aren't any empty seats.

II. Present Progressive: *Yes/No* Questions

Write the questions. Use the present progressive and the words in parentheses. Then complete the short answers.

1. (you/wear socks/today)

    A: _Are you wearing socks today?_ _____

    B: No, _____

2. (Mr. and Mrs. White/talk on the telephone right now)

    A: _____

    B: Yes, _____

3. (Juan/read a magazine/at this time)

    A: _____

    B: No, _____

4. (I/sit in your seat)

   A: _____

   B: Yes, _____

5. (you and I/do the right thing)

   A: _____

   B: Yes, _____

III. Present Progressive: *Yes/No* and *Wh-* Questions

Read the letter to Ko Chiang from Wei Liang.

Dear Ko Chiang,

How are you? My life here in Toronto is exciting. I'm studying English and meeting people from all over the world.

Right now it's snowing outside, and my room is very cold. I'm wearing a sweatshirt, wool pants, and boots. I'm still cold. My roommate, Pedro, is from Ecuador. He loves the snow and the cold. I hate it. Right now Pedro is skiing in the Laurentian Mountains. I'm dreaming about beaches and warm weather. How's the weather at home? Is it snowing?

Please write and tell me all about your life at school.

Regards to all,

Wei Liang

Now write the questions. Then answer them.

1. Where/Wei Liang

   A: Where is Wei Liang? _____

   B: _____

2. What/Wei Liang/do in Toronto

   A: _____

   B: _____

3. it/rain in Toronto now

   A: _____

   B: _____

4. What/Wei Liang/wear

   A: _____

   B: _____

5. Why/Wei Liang wear a sweatshirt, wool pants, and boots

    A: _____

    B: _____

6. What/Pedro/do now

    A: _____

    B: _____

7. Where/Pedro ski

    A: _____

    B: _____

8. Who/write a letter

    A: _____

    B: _____

IV. Synthesis: Error Correction

Correct these sentences.

1. What you doing? *What are you doing?* _____

2. We are stand near the bank now. _____

3. She wearing two sweaters because it's cold. _____

4. Who's talk on the phone? _____

5. Why they working on Sunday? _____

6. He laughing? _____

7. Who sit next to the window now? _____

8. She's crying why she's lonely. _____

9. We are eating and are drinking. _____

10. Is raining in Paris? _____

Unit 5: Final Test

I. Present Progressive: Affirmative and Negative Statements

Complete the sentences. Use the present progressive in the affirmative or negative. Use the words in the box.

cry	snow	take	watch
do	study	try	

1. Wear your boots. It ___'s snowing___ outside.

2. He's not home. He _____ at the library.

3 I _____ my taxes. I'm doing my math homework.

4. Smile. He _____ your picture.

5. I _____ because this book is sad.

6. Hurry. Look over there. Two men _____ to steal your car. Go after them.

7. They _____ TV because their TV is broken.

II. Present Progressive: *Yes/No* Questions

Write the questions. Use the present progressive and the words in parentheses. Then complete the short answers.

1. (it/rain)

   A: ___Is it raining_____ now?

   B: No, _____

2. (Dr. Smith/see patients)

   A: _____ now?

   B: Yes, _____

3. (we/land)

   A: _____

   B: Yes, _____ There's the airport.

4. (they/watch TV)

   A: _____

   B: No, _____ They're watching a video.

5. (the baby/wear a sweater)

   A: _____

   B: Yes, _____

III. Present Progressive: *Yes/No* and *Wh-* Questions

Read the letter to Juan from Maria.

Dear Juan,

Thanks for writing. I'm always happy to hear from you. My life here in San Francisco is very busy, but sometimes I'm still lonely for home. As you know, I'm working and studying. That's not easy. Two of my classes are interesting but difficult. One class is difficult. It's not interesting. My job is a lot of fun. I'm a salesperson in a big toy store. There are hundreds of toys in this store.

At the moment, I'm taking a break. It's raining, so I'm sitting in the back of the store. On nice days I take a walk.

I hope you and your family are fine. Say hi to everyone from me. Write soon.

Fondly,
Maria

Now write the questions. Then answer them.

1. Maria/work and study/in San Francisco this year

   A: Is Maria working and studying in San Francisco this year? _____

   B: _____

2. Maria/buy toys

   A: _____

   B: _____

3. How many classes/Maria/take

   A: _____

   B: _____

4. What/Maria/do/now

    A: _____

    B: _____

5. it/rain now

    A: _____

    B: _____

6. Where/Maria/sit

    A: _____

    B: _____

7. What/Maria/do/in the back of the store

    A: _____

    B: _____

8. Why/Maria/sit/in the back of the store

    A: _____

    B: _____

IV. Synthesis: Error Correction

Correct these sentences.

1. He's wearing a coat and a scarf why he's cold. He's wearing a coat and scarf because he's cold.

2. Where you living now? _____

3. She is watch a movie on TV. _____

4. He not selling his car. _____

5. I'm working, and am studying, too. _____

6. Why she is standing? _____

7. Who are listening to the radio now? _____

8. What she is doing? _____

9. Is snowing now? _____

10. What you studying? _____

Unit 6: Diagnostic Test

I. Simple Present Tense: Affirmative and Negative Statements

Complete the sentences. Use the simple present tense of the verbs in parentheses.

1. Every morning Mrs. Brown _____*goes*_____ to work at 8:00. She _____ a train and a bus.
   (go)   (take)

2. Mr. Brown _____ home and _____ the children.
   (stay)   (watch)

3. I _____ an umbrella, but I _____ a rain hat.
   (have)   (have, not)

4. They _____ the new buses. They _____ comfortable seats.
   (like, not)   (have, not)

5. It _____ a lot in the spring, but it rarely _____ in the summer.
   (rain)   (rain)

6. She _____ any milk. She _____ enough.
   (need, not)   (have)

7. I usually _____ a suit on weekdays. On weekends I _____ jeans.
   (wear)   (wear)

8. Mr. Johnson _____ at the university. He _____ physics.
   (work)   (teach)

9. It _____ in Saudi Arabia.
   (snow, not)

10. She _____ to school in July and August. She _____ to summer camp.
    (go, not)   (go)

II. Simple Present Tense: *Yes/No* Questions and Short Answers

Complete the questions and short answers. Use the simple present tense of the verbs in parentheses.

1. A: _____*Does*_____ he _____*need*_____ any wood?
                                (need)

   B: No, _____ .

2. A: _____ it _____ a lot to fly to Japan from New York?
                          (cost)

   B: Yes, _____ .

3. A: _____ they _____ German?
                           (speak)

   B: No, _____ .

4. A: _____ we _____ him?
                         (know)

   B: No, _____ .

5. A: _____ she _____ alone?
   (live)

   B: Yes, _____ .

6. A: _____ he usually _____ you after school?
   (visit)

   B: Yes, _____ .

7. A: _____ you _____ an English–English dictionary?
   (have)

   B: Yes, _____ .

8. A: _____ I _____ him?
   (know)

   B: No, you _____ . He's new here.

III. The Simple Present Tense: *Yes/No* Questions

Complete the questions. Use **Is, Are, Do**, *or* **Does.**

1. _____Is_____ the bathroom next to the bedrooms?

2. _____ your friends at the movies?

3. _____ your friends live near you?

4. _____ your car use a lot of gas?

5. _____ it warm outside today?

6. _____ sweatshirts cost a lot of money?

7. _____ there many teenagers at that pizza place?

8. _____ there a pizza place on the corner?

9. _____ Bill have an extra jacket?

10. _____ the Browns live on the second floor?

IV. Simple Present Tense: *Wh-* Questions

Read the sentences. Complete the questions and answer them. Use short answers.

1. He needs a new jacket because his old one has a big hole in it.

   A: Why _____does he need_____ a new jacket?

   B: _____

2. The boys usually study at the library.

   A: Where ——————————————————————

   B: ——————————————————————————

3. We exchange gifts on our birthdays.

   A: What ———————————————— on your birthdays?

   B: ——————————————————————————

4. My father loves to listen to opera.

   A: Who ——————————————————————

   B: ——————————————————————————

5. They eat a big meal in the evening.

   A: When ——————————————————————

   B: ——————————————————————————

6. I get up at 7:00 A.M.

   A: What time ——————————————————

   B: ——————————————————————————

7. He wears a suit and tie at his job.

   A: What ——————————————————————

   B: ——————————————————————————

8. They eat a lot of turkey because it's their favorite food.

   A: Why ——————————————————————

   B: ——————————————————————————

V. Questions with *Who* and *Who(m)*

Read the sentences. Then write questions about the subject and about the object.

1. Bob calls his family every Sunday.

   Who ——— *calls his family every Sunday?* ——— Bob does.

   Who(m) ——— *does he call?* ——— His family.

2. Mary visits her cousins once a month.

   Who —————————————————————————————— Mary does.

   Who(m) ————————————————————————————— Her cousins.

3. The teacher helps us with our homework.

   Who —————————————————————————————— The teacher does.

   Who(m) ————————————————————————————— Us.

4. That man often meets his friends in the park.

   Who —————————————————————————————— That man does.

   Who(m) ————————————————————————————— His friends.

VI. *This, That, These, Those*

*Complete the conversations. Use **this, that, these**, or **those**. Use capital letters where necessary.*

1. Doctor: Here. Take ——— *these* ——— pills three times a day.

   Patient: Thanks.

2. Sun Yeon: Look over there, across the street. ——————————'s my English teacher.

   Gioni: The one in the yellow sweater?

   Sun Yeon: Yes.

3. Bill: Hiro, —————————— is my friend, John. John, I want you to meet my brother, Hiro.

   John: Hi, Hiro.

   Hiro: Hi, John.

4. Janet: Ouch! —————————— nuts are hard. They're terrible.

   Russell: Don't eat any more. Throw them away.

   Janet: Good idea.

5. Salesman: —————————— dictionary in my hand costs $25.

   Customer: What about the one in the window?

   Salesman: —————————— one costs $15. —————————— dictionaries on the top shelf cost $9.

   Customer: Please show me the one in the window.

   Salesman: Sure. Just a minute.

   Customer: Thank you.

VII. *One, Ones,* and *It*

Change the underlined word or words to **one, ones**, *or* **it**. *Use capital letters where necessary.*

1. A: Where's your key?

   B: <u>My key</u>'s in my pocket. ⎯⎯ It ⎯⎯

2. A: How many watches does he own?

   B: Three. A gold <u>watch</u> and two silver <u>watches</u>. ⎯⎯⎯⎯⎯⎯

3. A: Where do you keep your pots?

   B: The big <u>pot</u> goes in the cabinet under the stove. The small <u>pots</u> go in the cabinet above the

   sink. ⎯⎯⎯⎯⎯⎯

4. A: What's your last name?

   B: <u>My last name</u> is Lee. ⎯⎯⎯⎯

5. A: We have white T-shirts and gray <u>T-shirts</u>. ⎯⎯⎯⎯

   B: How much are the white <u>T-shirts</u>? ⎯⎯⎯⎯

VIII. Synthesis: Error Correction

Correct these sentences.

1. We have green grapes and purple grapes. The green one are $1.99 a pound. ⎯⎯ We have green ⎯⎯

   grapes and purple grapes. The green ones are $1.99 a pound.

2. He doesn't goes to school on Saturday. ⎯⎯⎯⎯

3. It don't rain in the desert. ⎯⎯⎯⎯

4. These ones are navy, but this one is black. ⎯⎯⎯⎯

5. She doesn't lives in the city. ⎯⎯⎯⎯

6. Does she works in a hospital? ⎯⎯⎯⎯

7. When does he arrives? ⎯⎯⎯⎯

8. These film is sad. ⎯⎯⎯⎯

9. What time rises the sun? ⎯⎯⎯⎯

10. Who does live in that house? ⎯⎯⎯⎯

Unit 6: Final Test

I. Simple Present Tense: Affirmative and Negative Statements

Complete the sentences. Use the simple present tense of the verbs in parentheses.

1. I ___don't know___ him. I ___know___ his father.
   (know, not)   (know)

2. That woman _____ a scientist. She _____ at the university hospital.
              (be)   (work)

3. He _____ from Senegal. He _____ from the Ivory Coast.
      (be, not)   (come)

4. The bus _____ one dollar and twenty-five cents. You _____ exact change.
          (cost)   (need)

5. She _____ English, but she _____ it well.
      (understand)   (speak, not)

6. We usually _____ the news on TV. Sometimes we _____ a movie too.
             (watch)   (watch)

7. I _____ meat. I _____ a vegetarian.
    (eat, not)   (be)

8. Janet and Dan _____ tennis together on Sunday morning. Janet _____
                 (play)   (like)

   tennis. Dan _____ Janet.
               (like)

9. He _____ a car. He _____ the bus to his job.
      (have, not)   (take)

10. We often _____ after school and _____ out for coffee.
            (meet)   (go)

II. Simple Present Tense: *Yes/No* Questions and Short Answers

Complete the questions and short answers. Use the simple present tense of the verbs in parentheses.

1. A: ___Does___ he ___wear___ a hat in the winter?
                    (wear)

   B: No, ___he doesn't.___ . He never wears a hat.

2. A: _____ you _____ a new computer ribbon?
                      (need)

   B: Yes, _____ . My ribbon is worn.

3. A: _____ they _____ to the radio in the morning?
                       (listen)

   B: No, _____ . They don't have time.

4. A: ——————— it ——————— ?
   (hurt)

   B: No, ———————————. It feels fine.

5. A: ——————— we ——————— a date?
   (have)

   B: Yes, ———————————. We have a date for tomorrow at seven.

6. A: ——————— I ——————— time?
   (have)

   B: No, ———————————.

7. A: ——————— you ——————— the movie?
   (like)

   B: Yes, ———————————. Do you?

8. A: ——————— she ——————— Arabic?
   (speak)

   B: No, ———————————. Her father does.

III. Simple Present Tense: *Yes/No* Questions

Complete the questions. Use **Is, Are, Do**, *or* **Does**.

1. ____Do____ you love me?

2. ——————— you sure?

3. ——————— he have a comfortable seat?

4. ——————— lunch ready?

5. ——————— she at home?

6. ——————— it late?

7. ——————— you drive to the supermarket every week?

8. ——————— your friend enjoy golf?

9. ——————— they understand Turkish?

10. ——————— we early?

IV. Simple Present Tense: *Wh-* Questions

Read the sentences. Complete the questions and answer them. Use short answers.

1. He works because he needs money.

   A: Why *does he work?*

   B: *Because he needs the money.*

2. We begin class at nine o'clock.

   A: When _____

   B: _____

3. Sunday morning they play golf.

   A: When _____

   B: _____

4. They have breakfast at 8:30.

   A: What time _____

   B: _____

5. Our uncle has a house in the country.

   A: Who _____

   B: _____

6. He lives in the small house on the corner.

   A: Where _____

   B: _____

7. We watch TV after dinner.

   A: What _____

   B: _____

8. He wears those pants because they're comfortable.

A: Why _____

B: _____

V. Questions with *Who* and *Who(m)*

Read the sentences. Then write questions about the subject and about the object.

1. Joan meets classmates every day after class.

   Who _meets classmates every day after class?_____ Joan does.

   Who(m) _does Joan meet every day after class?_____ Classmates.

2. Jon writes his family once a month.

   Who _____ Jon does.

   Who(m) _____ His family.

3. That nurse helps patients with their showers.

   Who _____ That nurse does.

   Who(m) _____ Patients.

4. Ray calls his uncle after five o'clock.

   Who _____ Ray does.

   Who(m) _____ His uncle.

VI. *This, That, These, Those*

*Complete the conversations. Use **this, that, these,** or **those.***

1. A: Are ____these____ your gloves?

   B: Oh, yes. Thanks.

2. A: Who's _____ boy over there?

   B: I don't know. I think he's lost.

3. A: I don't understand _____ sentences in our book.

   B: I don't, either.

4. A: My birthday is on the tenth of ——————— month.

   B: That's next Monday. Happy Birthday.

5. A: I think ——————— men across the street are in danger.

   B: Let's go to them.

VII. *One, Ones, It*

*Change the underlined word or words to **one, ones**, or **it**.*

1. A: How many cats do they have?

   B: Three. A black <u>cat</u> and two black-and-white <u>cats</u>. *one, ones* _____

2. A: Is your dictionary in your bookbag?

   B: No, <u>my dictionary</u> is right here. _____

3. A: Where do I put the sheets?

   B: The white <u>sheets</u> go on the second shelf, and the blue <u>sheets</u> go on the top shelf. _____

4. A: Where's the men's room?

   B: <u>The men's room</u> is down the hall next to the water fountain. _____

   A: Thanks.

5. A: There are two toys. This <u>toy</u> is for Steve and this <u>toy</u> is for Andrea. _____

VIII. Synthesis: Error Correction

Correct these sentences.

1. Who does work at the library? *Who works at the library?* _____

2. Why does he steals? _____

3. These book is about grammar. _____

4. Does it rains a lot in Portland? _____

5. I lives alone. _____

6. We have a car. One is two years old. _____

7. Does she teaches every day? _____

8. That store don't open before ten o'clock. _____

9. This women are from Europe. _____

10. What time begins your class? _____

Unit 7: Diagnostic Test

I. Adverbs of Frequency/Expressions of Frequency

Rewrite the sentences. Add the word or words in parentheses to the sentences.

1. (every evening) He watches two or three hours of television . <u>Every evening he watches two or</u>

   <u>three hours of television.</u>

2. (often) I buy fruit at that market. _____

3. (rarely) We eat fish. _____

4. (always) He eats muffins with his dinner. _____

5. (three times a day) He takes these pills. _____

6. (usually) They are late. _____

II. Simple Present Tense and Present Progressive: *Wh-* Questions

Write questions in the simple present tense or present progressive. Use the words in parentheses.

1. (Where/he/run/now)

   _____ Where is he running now? _____

2. (How often/Mary and Joe/take a vacation)

   _____

3. (When/you/usually pay your rent)

   _____

4. (How often/he/go to the dentist)

   _____

5. (Why/we/eat at a restaurant today)

   _____

6. (What time/they/often eat breakfast)

_____

7. (What/she/wear to school/today)

_____

8. (What/you/want now)

_____

III. Contrast: Simple Present Tense and Present Progressive

Complete the conversations with the verbs in parentheses. Use the correct form of the simple present tense or the present progressive.

1. A: Look! There _____'s_____ John. He ___'s wearing___ a green jacket.
           (be)   (wear)

   B: Where _____ he? I _____ him.
             (be)   (see, not)

   A: He _____ behind that woman.
          (walk)

   B: Oh, now I _____ him.
               (see)

2. A: _____ you _____ any help with your homework?
                      (need)

   B: No, I _____ so. I _____ everything. This lesson isn't difficult.
            (think, not)   (understand)

   A: What _____ it about?
           (be)

   B: We _____ about the American Revolution.
         (learn)

3. A: Whose scarf _____ this?
                   (be)

   B: It _____ to Mary.
         (belong)

   A: Where _____ she?
            (be)

   B: She _____ at the library now.
          (study)

4. A: What _____ you _____ now?
   (do)

   B: I _____ on my stamp collection.
   (work)

   A: _____ you _____ any help?
   (want)

   B: Sure. Pull up a chair.

5. A: What _____ you _____ about the new computer?
   (think)

   B: I _____ it.
   (like)

   A: Who _____ it now?
   (use)

   B: The children. They _____ games on the computer.
   (play)

6. A: What _____ you usually _____ in the summer?
   (do)

   B: We _____ to the mountains every summer.
   (go)

   A: How long _____ you _____ there?
   (stay)

   B: About three or four weeks.

   A: That _____ wonderful.
   (sound)

IV. Verb + Noun or Infinitive

*Write sentences with the words in parentheses. Use the simple present tense
and the correct form of the verbs.*

1. (I/want/have/lunch now)

   I want to have lunch now.
   _____

2. (She/need/new glasses)

   _____

3. (We/like, not/drink/soda)

   _____

4. (We/prefer/juice)

   _____

V. Possessive Pronouns

Change the underlined words to possessive pronouns. Use **mine, his, hers, ours**, *or* **theirs**. *Use capital letters where necessary.*

1. A: Whose books are on the table?

   B: They aren't my books. ~~My books~~ Mine are in my bookbag.

2. A: What color eyes do they have?

   B: <u>Her eyes</u> are blue and <u>his eyes</u> are green.

3. A: Is this Ms. Green's class?

   B: No. <u>Her class</u> is in room 310.

4. A: Our class begins at 10:00. When does <u>your class</u> begin?

   B: At 11:00.

5. A: Is their apartment on the second floor?

   B: No. Their brother's apartment is on the second floor. <u>Their apartment</u> is on the third floor.

6. A: Our telephone isn't working. Is <u>your telephone</u> working?

   B: No, <u>our telephone</u> isn't, either.

VI. Synthesis: Error Correction

Correct these sentences.

1. I like play golf. <u>I like to play golf.</u>

2. They working at home. _____

3. Do you need go to the library? _____

4. She prefers to drinks coffee. _____

5. That's mine new umbrella. _____

6. What's yours brother's first name? _____

7. Right now she plays tennis. _____

8. He's owning a two bedroom apartment. _____

9. I'm agree. _____

10. I'm not believing you. _____

Unit 7: Final Test

I. Adverbs of Frequency/Expressions of Frequency

Rewrite the sentences. Add the word or words in parentheses to the sentences.

1. (always) He is on time. _____ He is always on time. _____

2. (always) She wears a red hat. _____

3. (twice a week) They water those plants. _____

4. (once in a while) We drive to the mountains. _____

5. (rarely) You help with the housework. _____

6. (often) It rains in April. _____

II. Simple Present Tense and Present Progressive: *Wh-* Questions

Write questions in the simple present tense or present progressive. Use the words in parentheses.

1. (How often/you/eat spaghetti)

   _____ How often do you eat spaghetti? _____

2. (How often/she/call you)

   _____

3. (How often/they/write to you)

   _____

4. (Where/they/usually go/in the evening)

   _____

5. (Why/he/cry/now)

   _____

6. (Who/own/that big house)

   _____

7. (When/ your friend/ usually take a vacation)

   _____

8. (Where/Jack and Joanne/play/at this moment)

   _____

III. Contrast: Simple Present Tense and Present Progressive

Complete the conversations with the verbs in parentheses. Use the correct form of the simple present tense or the present progressive.

1. A: _____Do_____ you _____like_____ the new trains?

   B: Yes. They _'re_____ fast, comfortable, and quiet.
   (be)

2. A: What _____ Jack _____ now?
   (do)

   B: He _____ a composition.
   (write)

   A: _____ he usually _____ his homework at night?
   (do)

   B: Yes, he does.

3. A: _____ you _____ the Shinoharas?
   (know)

   B: Yes. We _____ in the same building.
   (live)

   A: Well, Mrs. Shinohara _____ on TV now. She _____ about a student-
   (be)   (talk)

   exchange program.

4. A: _____ Josh _____ dinner?
   (cook)

   B: Not today. Today Pete _____ . Josh _____ on Monday and Wednesday.
   (cook)   (cook)

   Pete _____ on Tuesday and Thursday. On Friday, Saturday, and Sunday they
   (cook)

   _____ . They _____ in restaurants.
   (cook, not)   (eat)

5. A: Mmm. These grapes _____ delicious.
   (be)

   B: I _____ . Do we _____ more?
   (agree)   (have)

   A: No.

   B: Too bad.

6. A: Look. Those boys _____ .
   (fight)

   B: They _____ . They _____ .
   (fight, not)   (play)

   A: Oh, you're right.

IV. Verb + Noun or Infinitive

Write sentences with the words in parentheses. Use the simple present tense and the correct form of the verbs.

1. (They/like/go/to the park)

    _____ They like to go to the park. _____

2. (He/need/a new watch)

    _____

3. (I/prefer/stay home today)

    _____

4. (She/want/a red carpet)

    _____

V. Possessive Pronouns

*Change the underlined words to possessive pronouns. Use **mine, his, hers, ours,** or **theirs**. Use capital letters where necessary.*

1. A: Whose wallet is this?

    B: It's ~~her wallet~~.   *hers*

2. A: Is that your pen?

    B: No. <u>My pen</u> is blue. That one is black.

3. A: My seat number is M102. What's <u>your seat number</u>?

    B: <u>My seat number</u> is M104.

4. A: Is his jacket on the bed?

    B: No. <u>His jacket</u> is in the closet.

5. A: Our class has twenty students. Is your class big, too?

    B: No. <u>Our class</u> is small. There are only nine students in it.

6. A: Is this his wallet?

    B: No. It's <u>her wallet</u>.

VI. Synthesis: Error Correction

Correct these sentences.

1. Once in a while I'm wearing jeans. *Once in a while I wear jeans.*

2. Always I eat a big breakfast. _____

3. Mine eyes are blue. _____

4. She prefers play tennis. _____

5. I'm needing a new tennis racket. _____

6. How often you paint your apartment? _____

7. Right now we polish the furniture. _____

8. I'm agree with you. _____

9. I want study physics. _____

10. He need to find a new apartment. _____

Unit 8: Diagnostic Test

I. Simple Present Tense: Affirmative and Negative Statements

Complete the sentences in the affirmative or negative of the simple past tense.
Use the verbs in parentheses.

1. Last night we ____cooked____ a big meal, but the day before yesterday we ____ate____ at a
   (cook)   (eat)

   restaurant.

2. Yesterday I _____ John. I _____ him.
   (call)   (visit, not)

3. Walter's in the hospital. He _____ off a swing and _____ his arm.
   (fall)   (break)

4. We _____ to school yesterday. Susan's boyfriend _____ us.
   (walk, not)   (drive)

5. Yesterday morning I _____ an apple pie. We _____ it last night.
   (bake)   (finish)

6. My friends and I _____ a football game on TV. We _____ football in the
   (watch, not)   (play)

   park.

7. We _____ at eleven o'clock yesterday morning. Then we _____ a train to
   (meet)   (take)

   the city and _____ a play.
   (see)

8. I'm not thirsty. I _____ two cups of tea before we _____ .
   (drink)   (leave)

9. Yesterday morning he _____ the bus and _____ to school twenty minutes
   (miss)   (come)

   late.

10. Last Sunday they _____ to the park and _____ tennis for three hours.
    (go)   (play)

II. Past Tense Markers

*Complete the sentences. Use **last, ago,** or **yesterday**. Use capital letters where*
necessary.

1. ____Last____ night I visited him at the hospital.

2. I worked at a bank three years _____ .

3. _____ he called me.

4. _____ week we invited them to the party.

5. _____ morning I borrowed his sweater.

III. Simple Past Tense: *Yes/No* and *Wh-* Questions

Complete the conversations. Use the correct form of the verbs in parentheses.

1. A: Why is Mary waiting outside? _____Did_____ she _____forget_____ her key?
   (forget)

   B: I think so. She probably _____ bags and _____ her keys in her other bag.
   (change)   (leave)

2. A: Where _____ they _____ last night?
   (go)

   B: John _____ basketball, and Phil _____ to a party.
   (play)   (go)

3. A: What _____ the children _____ for dinner?
   (eat)

   B: Andrea _____ spaghetti and Billy _____ meatballs.
   (eat)   (have)

4. A: _____ you _____ my report?
   (read)

   B: Oh yes. I _____ it twice.
   (read)

5. A: _____ she _____ a cake to the office yesterday?
   (bring)

   B: No. She _____ a dozen donuts.
   (bring)

IV. Questions with *Who* and *Who(m)*

Read the sentences. Then complete the questions.

1. Sally met Tom.

   Who _____met Tom?_____ Sally did.

   Who(m) _____did Sally meet?_____ Tom.

2. My friends helped that older man.

   Who _____ My friends did.

   Who(m) _____ That older man.

3. Maria called her father on Sunday.

   Who _____ Maria did.

   Who(m) _____ Her father.

V. Contrast: Simple Present, Present Progressive, and Simple Past Tense

Complete the conversations. Use the simple present, present progressive, or past tense. Use the correct form of the verb in parentheses.

1. A: It's warm here. Why _____*are*_____ you _____*wearing*_____ a sweater?
                                                        (wear)

   B: I _____ well. I _____ cold. I _____ the flu a couple of days
           (feel, not)   (be)   (catch)

   ago.

2. A: _____ you _____ your homework last night?
                            (finish)

   B: No. I _____ it right now.
                 (finish)

3. A: _____ they _____ a car?
                            (have)

   B: Yes, they do. They _____ one last month. Right now they _____ to
                              (buy)   (drive)

   Washington, D.C.

4. A: _____ the boy _____ now because he _____ his money?
                                (cry)   (lose)

   B: Yes, I think so.

5. A: Look. There's your uncle. He _____ soccer with those men.
                                        (play)

   B: I know. My uncle always _____ soccer on Sunday morning.
                                    (play)

   He _____ a soccer club last spring.
         (join)

   A: He _____ good.
            (be)

VI. Synthesis: Error Correction

Correct these sentences.

1. Who did works at the library last night? <u>Who worked at the library last night?</u>

2. Did they baked a cake? _____

3. She go to San Francisco on vacation two months ago. _____

4. Before two weeks we returned that chair. _____

5. What happen at the party last night? _____

6. Did it rained during the ball game? _____

7. We didn't visited the museum. _____

8. What you borrowed from your friend? _____

Unit 8: Final Test

I. Simple Past Tense: Affirmative and Negative Statements

Complete the sentences in the affirmative or negative of the simple past tense.
Use the verbs in parentheses.

1. Yesterday I _____spoke_____ to my boss and _____ for a raise.
   (speak)   (ask)

2. We _____ the present because they _____ it.
   (find, not)   (hide)

3. I'm sorry. I _____ your name.
   (forget)

4. He _____ in the last war. Fortunately, he _____ hurt.
   (fight)   (get, not)

5. They _____ hard and _____ rich in a short time.
   (work)   (become)

6. I feel bad. I _____ twenty dollars from my friend last month, and I _____ to
   (borrow)   (forget)

   give it back.

7. She _____ the teacher, so she _____ him for help.
   (understand, not)   (ask)

8. I _____ a lot of homework yesterday. I _____ two compositions and
   (do)   (write)

   _____ three chapters of chemistry.
   (read)

9. I _____ my vest because it _____ a stain.
   (wear, not)   (have)

10. We _____ the door open and someone _____ a computer from our office.
    (leave)   (steal)

II. Past Tense Markers

*Complete the sentences. Use **last, ago**, or **yesterday**. Use capital letters where*
necessary.

1. Three weeks _____ago_____ they discovered a new way to get home.

2. _____ afternoon we listened to music for a few hours.

3. _____ week I lost my voice.

4. _____ night we watched a very funny movie on TV.

5. She bought her computer several years _____.

III. Simple Past Tense: *Yes/No* and *Wh-* Questions

Complete the conversations. Use the correct form of the verbs in parentheses.

1. A: _____Did_____ they _____finish_____ the job?
                                        (finish)

   B: Oh yes. They _____ it about an hour ago.
                              (finish)

2. A: Who _____ all the bread?
                    (eat)

   B: I did.

3. A: When _____ she _____ her bracelet.
                                              (lose)

   B: She _____ it. Someone _____ it.
              (lose, not)   (steal)

4. A: Who _____ you _____?
                                      (call)

   B: My brother. I _____ him about my new job.
                          (tell)

5. A: Where _____ they _____ that lamp?
                                            (buy)

   B: They _____ it. Their friend _____ it to them.
              (buy, not)   (give)

   A: That's a nice friend.

IV. Questions with *Who* and *Who(m)*

Read the sentences. Then complete the questions.

1. Emiko visited her aunt on Mother's Day.

   Who _____ visited her aunt on Mother's Day? _____ Emiko did.

   Who(m) _____ did Emiko visit on Mother's Day? _____ Her aunt.

2. The boys met their teacher at the park.

   Who _____ The boys did.

   Who(m) _____ Their teacher.

3. Bill saw his mother at the supermarket.

   Who _____ Bill did.

   Who(m) _____ His mother.

V. Contrast: Simple Present, Present Progressive, and Simple Past Tense

Complete the conversations. Use the simple present, present progressive, or past tense. Use the correct form of the verb in parentheses.

1. A: When _____did_____ you _____catch_____ that fish?
   (catch)

   B: At six o'clock this morning.

   A: What _____ you _____ with the fish now?
   (do)

   B: I _____ it. Would you like to join me for lunch?
   (clean)

   A: No, thanks. I _____ fish.
   (hate)

2. A: Those beads are beautiful. What _____ you _____ with them?
   (make)

   B: I'm trying to make a pair of earrings. Last week I _____ a necklace.
   (make)

   A: I _____ it on you yesterday. You _____ a terrific job.
   (see)   (do)

   B: Thanks.

3. A: _____ it _____ last night?
   (rain)

   B: No, but it _____ now. _____ you _____ an umbrella?
   (rain)   (have)

   A: No, but I _____ a raincoat and a rainhat.
   (have)

4. A: Who _____ history last year?
   (teach)

   B: Ms. Mahler. Everyone _____ her class.
   (love)

   A: _____ she _____ a lot of work?
   (give)

   B: Yes, but we _____ a lot.
   (learn)

5. A: We usually _____ football, but today we _____ football because it was
   (play)   (play, not)

   too hot.

   B: _____ you _____ football yesterday?
   (play)

   A: Yes, we did.

VIII. Synthesis: Error Correction

Correct these sentences.

1. Before three days he took that test. *Three days ago he took that test.*

2. Did you ate turkey last night? _____

3. It didn't worked. _____

4. Why you came late this morning? _____

5. When began the movie? _____

6. Do we have a test last week? _____

7. Two weeks ago the men did worked on the bridge? _____

8. Who find the book last night? _____

Unit 9: Diagnostic Test

I. Present and Past Tenses: Affirmative with *Be*

Complete the sentences with **'s, 'm, 're, was,** *or* **were.**

1. Time flies. Last year my son _____was_____ in junior high school. Now he _____ in high school.

2. Last year we _____ students. Now we _____ teachers.

3. My wife and I work at a hospital. I _____ a nurse, and my wife _____ a doctor.

4. My friends _____ at the restaurant at seven o'clock, but now they _____ on their way home.

5. Take off your jacket. It _____ hot and humid.

II. *Yes/No* Questions: Past and Present

Complete the questions. Use **Is, Are, Am, Was, Were, Do, Does,** *or* **Did**.

1. _____Did_____ you get your pay check yesterday afternoon?

2. Jack wasn't home last night. _____ he at the office?

3. _____ you tired? There's an extra bed over there.

4. _____ they usually eat cereal in the morning? They're staying with me so I need to know.

5. _____ it cost a lot to live in your city these days?

6. _____ many students late to class yesterday morning?

7. _____ your watch working now?

8. _____ he break his arm last Tuesday?

9. _____ your parents at the airport last Monday?

10. _____ I still the secretary?

III. Past Tense: *Wh*-Questions

Write questions in the past tense. Use the words in parentheses.

1. (Who/be late/last week)

    A: _____

    B: Russell was.

2. (Where/he/buy/those paintings)

    A: _____

    B: At a gallery on Madison Avenue.

3. (When/they/be in Paris)

    A: _____

    B: Three years ago.

4. (Why/she/wear/a long skirt)

    A: _____

    B: Because she went to a party at her boss's home.

5. (How/be/your classes/last year)

    A: _____

    B: Interesting, but a lot of work.

6. (What/be/your favorite game as a child)

    A: _____

    B: I liked to play checkers.

7. (What/you/do/yesterday after school)

    A: _____

    B: Nothing. I went home and went to sleep.

IV. *There is/There are/There was/There were*: Affirmative and Negative Statements and *Yes/No* Questions

Complete the conversations. Choose from the words in the box.

There's	There isn't	There are	There aren't
There was	There wasn't	There were	There weren't
Is there	Are there	Was there	Were there

1. A: Why were you so late?

    B: _____There weren't_____ any buses. We walked all the way here.

    A: That was a long walk.

2. A: _____ a storm last night?

   B. Yes. A big tree fell on my neighbor's house.

3. A: Don't be surprised. _____ a cat under the table.

   B: Thanks for telling me. I thought it was you.

4. A: _____ any grapes in the refrigerator? I'm in the mood for grapes.

   B: Yes. I bought a pound of grapes yesterday afternoon.

5. A: _____ any matches on the stove?

   B: No, but John had a lighter in his pocket.

6. A: We never drive downtown. _____ any parking spaces there. We always

   use public transportation.

   B: That's smart.

7. A: _____ any juice, so I drank water.

   B: Oh.

8. A: Why was the line so long?

   B: _____ a big sale.

V. Past Tense: Regular and Irregular Past Tense Forms

Complete the sentences. Use the simple past tense of the verbs in parentheses.

1. I __didn't borrow__ the book. I _____ it.
      (borrow, not)   (buy)

2. She _____ a cold last week and _____ two days of work.
        (catch)   (miss)

3. They _____ us at the park. Then we _____ to a restaurant together.
        (meet)   (go)

4. The children _____ ponies.
        (ride)

5. We _____ class at 10:30 and _____ at 12:30.
      (begin)   (finish)

6. I like your new sweater. Who _____ it?
               (choose)

7. She _____ the ball. She _____ it.
     (kick, not)   (throw)

8. We _____ letters to the editor of the local newspaper.
      (write)

9. They _____ castles in the sand.
   (build)

10. They _____ him at first, but now they do.
    (understand, not)

VI. Synthesis: Error Correction

Correct these sentences.

1. Did you be late? _Were you late?_ _____

2. Were she at the movies last night? _____

3. Today we was busy. _____

4. They was at a party at the International Center. _____
   _____

5. Was there any questions at the end of his speech? _____
   _____

6. Who's late yesterday? _____

7. When did they be in class last week? _____

8. There weren't a cup in the kitchen. _____

9. There wasn't any erasers in the classroom. _____
   _____

10. Where was you this morning? _____

Unit 9: Final Test

I. Present and Past Tenses: Affirmative with *Be*

Complete the sentences with **'s, 'm, 're, was,** *or* **were**.

1. People change. He _____was_____ a nervous child. But now he _____ a relaxed adult.

2. Last week all the peaches _____ hard. This week they _____ soft.

3. It _____ a beautiful day. The sun is shining and the birds are singing.

4. Yesterday they _____ at the beach, and the day before that they _____ at a

   concert. Now they _____ home.

5. I _____ tired, and I have a headache.

II. *Yes/No* Questions: Past and Present

Complete the questions. Use **Is, Are, Am, Was, Were, Do, Does,** *or* **Did**.

1. _____Did_____ you find your keys last night?

2. _____ he still sick now?

3. _____ there a storm a week ago?

4. _____ I the first one to speak?

5. _____ the boys early yesterday?

6. _____ she usually work on Sundays these days?

7. _____ you know his address by heart. I don't.

8. _____ you ready? Everyone is here.

9. _____ you upset when he lied?

10. _____ they buy any clothes at the flea market last week?

III. Past tense: *Wh-* Questions

Write questions in the past tense. Use the words in parentheses.

1. (When/you/visit/San Francisco)

   A: _____When did you visit San Francisco?_____

   B: Three years ago. We stayed there for a week.

2. (Who/be/with you/on your trip last month)

   A: _____

   B: My friend and my cousin.

3. (What/they/see/at the museum/yesterday)

   A: _____

   B: Mostly paintings and sculptures.

4. (When/be/he/at the library)

   A: _____

   B: From about seven to nine last night.

5. (How/be/your first day at work)

   A: _____

   B: Very busy. I didn't have time for lunch.

6. (Where/she/get/those boots)

   A: _____

   B: She bought them at a small store in the country.

7. (Why/be/they/angry last night)

   A: _____

   B: Because their friend forgot to meet them, and they waited for him for over an hour.

IV. *There is/There are/There was/There were*: Affirmative and Negative Statements and *Yes/No* Questions

Complete the conversations. Choose from the words in the box.

There's	There isn't	There are	There aren't
There was	There wasn't	There were	There weren't
Is there	Are there	Was there	Were there

1. A: _____Are there_____ any clean towels in the closet?

   B: Yes. Here's one.

2. A: Look! _____ a beautiful blue bird on the terrrace.

   B: Shh. I see it. Let's try and feed it.

3. A: _____ a doctor in the house? My friend is very sick.

   B: I'm a doctor. What seems to be the matter?

4. A: _____ a fire? There were five firemen in the building.

   B: No, It was a false alarm.

5. A: _____ any problems in your biology class yesterday?

   B: No, why do you ask?

6. A: Did you buy any cherries?

   B: No. _____ any good cherries at this time of the year.

7. A: Is your class big?

   B: No. _____ only ten students in it.

8. A: Why are the cars wet?

   B: _____ a rain storm early this morning.

V. Past Tense: Regular and Irregular Past Tense Forms

Complete the sentences. Use the simple past tense of the verbs in parentheses.

1. Yesterday the children __*didn't ride*__ horses. They _____ camels.
   (ride, not)   (ride)

2. We had a wonderful meal. We _____ sushi and _____ cranberry juice.
                               (eat)   (drink)

3. My aunt and uncle _____ to visit us for a week and _____ for three months.
                      (come)   (stay)

4. They _____ and _____ at the same time.
         (laugh)   (cry)

5. She _____ a lot of money on clothes. She _____ money on food.
         (spend)   (spend, not)

6. We _____ wool sweaters and wool scarves, but we _____ jackets.
      (wear)   (wear, not)

7. She _____ her nephew to school with her. He _____ a very nice time.
         (bring)   (have)

8. We _____ and _____ two articles from the newspaper in class yesterday.
      (read)   (discuss)

9. I _____ a postcard to my friend in Canada.
     (write)

10. We _____ them very well before this year.
       (know, not)

VI. Synthesis: Error Correction

Correct these sentences.

1. They were three policemen in front of our school yesterday. ___There were three policemen___ in front of our school yesterday.

2. Did you be on time last Monday? _____

3. When was you at the doctor last year? _____

4. Next year they were in the third year of high school. _____

   _____

5. What was you afraid of? _____

6. There wasn't any lemons in the refrigerator. _____

7. Were she the teacher last year, too? _____

8. Who be here last night? _____

9. I were at the library from nine to three yesterday. _____

   _____

10. When was there problems? _____

Unit 10: Diagnostic Test

I. Indefinite Articles and Quantifiers: *A, An, Some, A little, A few, Several, Much,* and *Many*

Complete each sentence with the correct word in parentheses.

1. I need _____*some*_____ information about Canada's population.
   (an, some)

2. We bought _____ chairs at the department store.
   (some, much)

3. He's _____ hour late.
   (a, an)

4. _____ people never come on time.
   (Some, Any)

5. She needs _____ help.
   (a little, a few)

6. I made _____ mistakes.
   (a little, a few)

7. She didn't have _____ problems at the office.
   (any, some)

8. They didn't buy _____ cheese.
   (any, some)

9. She has _____ cousins in the United States.
   (much, many)

10. _____ window was open.
    (One, Several)

II. Count and Non-count Nouns

Some of the underlined words are correct. Others take a plural form. Change the nouns to the plural form where necessary.

      meatballs
1. He ate ~~meatball~~ and rice.
2. She's a language teacher.
3. Several sweatshirt were on sale.
4. Their money is in an envelope.
5. There aren't any bowl in the cabinet.
6. He has lots of time.
7. We bought some milk and egg.
8. These chair are very comfortable.
9. The waitress are fast and friendly.
10. We have a lot of good friend at school.

III. *How much/How many*

Complete the conversations. Use **How much** *or* **How many**.

1. A: _____How many_____ women are there in your class?

   B: Twelve.

2. A: We need some juice.

   B: _____ do you need?

3. A: _____ gallons of gas does your gas tank take?

   B: I'm not sure.

4. A: _____ homework do you get each night?

   B: It varies from day to day.

5. A: She bought a lot of sweaters.

   B: _____ did she buy?

6. A: _____ does a good stereo cost?

   B: A thousand dollars.

   A: Wow!

IV. **Measure Words**

Complete the sentences. Use the words in the box.

roll	pound	cup
quart	teaspoon	tube

1. Let's get a _____roll_____ of film before we leave for Europe.

2. Those grapes cost two dollars a _____ .

3. I need to buy a _____ of milk.

4. She drank a _____ of tea.

5. I use a _____ of sugar in my coffee.

6. Please don't forget to buy a _____ of toothpaste.

V. Enough + Noun/*Too much/Too many/Too few/Too little*

Complete each sentence with the correct word in parentheses.

1. We have _____ *too much* _____ homework. Please don't give us anymore.
   (too much, too little)

2. Put that desk in the basement. We don't have _____ room for it here.
   (enough, too much)

3. That costs _____ money. We can't afford it.
   (enough, too much)

4. There's _____ time to finish the job.
   (too much, too little)

5. I don't like this fish. There are _____ bones in it.
   (too many, too few)

6. She couldn't graduate because she took _____ courses.
   (too little, too few)

VI. Modals: *Can/Could, May/Can, Would like/Would you like*

Complete the conversations. Choose from the sentences in the box.

```
May I help you?
Could I please borrow your pen?
I can't understand him.
Could you please help me carry these boxes?
No, but I'd like some coffee.
I couldn't understand him.
```

1. A: Do you want any dessert?

   B: _____ No, but I'd like some coffee. _____

2. A: _____?

   B: Yes, please. I'm looking for a pair of leather boots.

3. A: What's the problem?

   B: _____ He talks too fast.

4. A: _____?

   B: Sure. Here it is.

5. A: _____?

   B: I'd like to, but I have a bad back.

6. A: What was the problem?

   B: _____

VII. Synthesis: Error Correction

Correct these sentences.

1. Could you please to find your seats? *Could you please find your seats?* _____

2. Where would you like go? _____

3. How much people went to the game? _____

4. There weren't students enough to have a class. _____

   _____

5. She can types sixty words a minute. _____

6. How many roll of film did you buy? _____

7. Did she give us a lot of homeworks? _____

8. How many cup of coffees did you drink? _____

9. What would she likes to do after lunch? _____

10. There's a few problem in your report. _____

Unit 10: Final Test

I. Indefinite Articles and Quantifiers: *A, An, Some, A little, A few, Several, Much,* and *Many*

Complete each sentence with the correct word in parentheses.

1. We moved _____some_____ furniture from the basement to the attic.
   (a, some)

2. Did you buy _____ souvenirs on your last trip?
   (much, many)

3. _____ door had a sign on it.
   (Several, One)

4. There was only _____ work left.
   (a little, a few)

5. It took us _____ minutes to find our jackets.
   (a little, a few)

6. They don't know _____ foreign languages.
   (any, some)

7. She attends _____ university in Pennsylvania.
   (a, an)

8. We visited _____ interesting places in Europe.
   (some, much)

9. It didn't cost _____ money to go there by bus.
   (much, many)

10. Put _____ water on the fire.
    (a, some)

II. Count and Non-count Nouns

Some of the underlined nouns are correct. Others take a plural form. Change the nouns to the plural form where necessary.

1. She is studying <u>history</u> and <u>music</u>.   correct
2. The <u>mail</u> is late.
3. Please don't forget to buy <u>milk</u>, orange <u>juice</u>, and <u>cheese</u>.
4. Those <u>chair</u> are comfortable.
5. That <u>lamp</u> is very interesting but it doesn't give much <u>light</u>.
6. My <u>shoe</u> are under the bed.
7. I need a <u>frame</u> for this <u>picture</u>.
8. The <u>party</u> is at eight o'clock.
9. We cooked some <u>fish</u> and <u>rice</u> for dinner.
10. He found some <u>magazine</u> in an old suitcase.

III. *How much/How many*

Complete the conversations. Use **How much** *or* **How many**.

1. A: _____How much_____ water did you use to make the soup?

   B: Two quarts.

2. A: _____ days are there in September?

   B: Thirty.

3. A: _____ time does it take to get to Washington, D.C. from New York City.

   B: About four and a half hours by car.

4. A: _____ gas did you put in the car?

   B: Ten gallons.

5. A: _____ ways can you solve that problem?

   B: Only one way.

6. A: _____ does it cost to call Florida?

   B: It depends on the time of day.

IV. Measure Words

Complete the sentences. Use the words in the box.

glass	gallon	bowl
roll	pound	tablespoon

1. I'm thirsty. Could you get me a _____glass_____ of water.

2. My family drinks a lot of juice. I buy a _____ of juice every other day.

3. I use a _____ of chopped meat, an egg, an onion, and some salt in the meatloaf.

4. When he spilled the soda, he used a _____ of paper towels to clean up the mess.

5. I usually eat a _____ of soup at dinner time.

6. When I make an apple pie, I only add a _____ of sugar to the filling.

V. *Enough + Noun/Too much/Too many/Too few/Too little*

Complete each sentence with the correct word in parentheses.

1. There isn't _____enough_____ time for her to speak.
   (enough, too much)

2. There are _____ cooks in the kitchen.
   (too much, too many)

3. I bought _____ apples. Would you like to take some home?
   (too few, too many)

4. Add some more people to your painting. There are _____ people in it.
   (too little, too few)

5. Two people lost their jobs. There was _____ work.
   (too little, too few)

6. There weren't _____ chairs for everyone to sit.
   (enough, too much)

VI. Modals: *Can/Could, May/Can, Would like/Would you like*

Complete the conversations. Choose from the sentences in the box.

> Yes. I'd like some strawberries and cream, please.
> How can I get to the library from here?
> May I borrow your pen?
> I couldn't find mine.
> Would you like to dance?
> Can you type?

1. A: Would you like to dance? _____

   B: I'm sorry. I hurt my ankle.

2. A: _____ ? I forgot mine at home.

   B: Sure. Here.

3. A: _____ ?

   B: Yes, but not very quickly, only about twenty words a minute.

4. A: _____ ?

   B: Take the number 4 bus and get off at 50th Street. It's right there.

5. A: Do you care for dessert?

   B: _____ .

6. A: Why did you wear Dad's jacket?

   B: _____ .

VII. Synthesis: Error Correction

Correct these sentences.

1. We bought a little bananas at the store. We bought a few bananas at the store. _____

2. We did our homeworks together. _____

3. Could I please to see your report? _____

4. How much juices did they drink? _____

5. I'd like visit them next week. _____

6. She has much relatives in this country. _____

   _____

7. Please don't buy some fruit. _____

8. She can skis very well. _____

9. We saw a few snow on the top of the mountain. _____

   _____

10. Several student stayed home last Monday. _____

    _____

Unit 11: Diagnostic Test

I. *Be Going to* for the Future: Affirmative and Negative Statements

Complete the sentences with the affirmative or negative forms of **be going to** *for the future. Use the words in parentheses.*

1. Jane is sick.

   (see the doctor) She *'s going to see the doctor.* _____

   (go to school) She _____

2. Jamie has a test Tuesday morning.

   (study all day Monday) He _____

   (study Tuesday night) He _____ He's going to go to a party.

3. It's raining hard.

   (go on a picnic) We _____

   (stay home and watch videos) We_____

4. The Smiths have four children. They live in a small apartment in the city. They don't like the city.

   (stay in the city) _____

   (buy a house and move to the country)_____

5. I'm tired.

   (watch that movie) _____

   (go to sleep)_____

II. Contrast: *Be Going to* for the Future and Simple Past

Complete the sentences with the correct form of the verb in parentheses. Use **be going to** *for the future or the simple past tense.*

1. Last year she ____*went*____ to school part time and _____
   (go) (work)

   part time. Next year she _____ to school full time.
   (go)

2. Yesterday I _____ apples. I _____ my friend two bags
   (pick) (give)

   of apples. Tomorrow afternoon she _____ an apple pie.
   (bake)

3. Gail _____ here later today. I _____ to her earlier, and
   (come) (speak)

   she _____ me she would like to see us.
   (tell)

4. You _____ reading those books last week. They're due tomorrow. When
   (finish)

_____ you _____ them?
                        (return)

5. I feel terrible. I _____ my leather gloves. I _____
                        (lose)   (buy)

another pair of gloves tomorrow, but this time I _____ wool gloves, not
                                                    (buy)

leather ones.

III. Present Progressive for the Future

Complete the conversation with the correct form of the verb in parentheses.
Use the present progressive for the future.

A: What's his schedule?

B: He ___'s leaving___ New York on Tuesday. He _____ to Baltimore in the early after-
        1. (leave)   2. (fly)

noon. After a meeting in Baltimore, he _____ a train to Washington, D.C. Then,
                                          3. (take)

Wednesday night, he _____ to Atlanta, and Thursday night he _____ to New
                        4. (fly)   5. (return)

York.

A: Who _____ for all these flights?
        6. (pay)

B: Who knows? All I know is I _____ for them.
                                7. (pay, not)

IV. *Will* for the Future: Affirmative and Negative Statements

*Complete the conversations. Use the affirmative or negative of **will** and the words in parentheses.*

1. A: Don't worry. (It/hurt) ___It won't hurt._____

   B: Are you sure, Doctor?

2. A: My bags are very heavy.

   B: (I/help/you) _____

3. A: I have a late night meeting. (I/be/home/until 10:00 P.M.) _____

   B: I'll save some food.

4. A: Please wait for me. (I/be/back in five minutes) _____

   B: Okay.

5. A: He's very stubborn. (He/apologize) _____

   B: That's terrible.

V. Contrast: *May/Might/Will*

Choose the correct word or words in parentheses to complete the conversations.

1. A: Where are you going this afternoon?

   B: I'm not sure. I _____may_____ visit my friend in the hospital.
   (may, 'll)

2. A: Sometimes there's traffic on Friday afternoons. We _____ be a few minutes late.
   (might, will)

   B: Don't worry. We _____ be here all day.
   (may, 'll)

3. A: I'm looking for a carpet. Where can I find one?

   B: I don't know. Look in the paper. There _____ be some ads for carpets.
   (may, will)

4. A: Hurry. I don't want to be late.

   B: Don't worry. We _____ be late.
   (might not, won't)

5. A: John's going to meet us at 2:00.

   B: Maybe he _____ and maybe he _____ . With John you can never be
   (may, will)   (may not, won't)

   sure.

VI. Verb Tense Forms: Simple Present Tense, Present Progressive, Simple Past Tense, *Be Going to* for the Future, *Will* for the Future

Complete the sentences. Use the correct form of the following words in each sentence. In some cases there is more than one correct answer.

John/write/a letter

1. Yesterday _John wrote a letter._ _____

2. Right now _____

3. Is _____ at this moment?

4. Did _____ last week?

5. Is _____ tomorrow?

6. Will _____ next week?

7. Is _____ now?

8. Does _____ twice a week?

Simple Present Tense, Present Progressive, Simple Past Tense,
VII. *Be Going to* and *Will* for the Future

Complete the conversations. Use the correct form of the verb in parentheses.

1. A: What _____are_____ you _____doing_____ now?
                                (do)

   B: I _____ for a math test.
          (study)

   A: It _____ hard to study in the summer.
          (be)

   B: You're right. I'm hot and I'm hungry. I _____ a break and get a sandwich at the
                                                (take)

      coffee shop on the corner. _____ you hungry?
                                      (Be)

   A: Yes. I _____ you in five minutes.
              (join)

2. A: There _____ a big sale on towels yesterday. _____ you
              (be)

      _____ any?
          (buy)

   B: Yes. I _____ five bath towels, but I _____ them later today.
              (buy)   (return)

   A: Why?

   B: There _____ some stains on the towels.
              (be)

   A: That's too bad.

3. A: When _____ the mail usually _____ ?
                                            (come)

   B: At about noon.

   A: It's 12:30. I _____ the mailbox.
                    (check)

   B: What _____ you _____ for?
                              (wait)

   A: A check. My friend _____ $100 last week. He _____ me the check's in
                          (borrow)   (tell)

      the mail.

   B: Good luck.

4. A: I'm so nervous.

   B: Why?

   A: Today is my son's first day in kindergarten.

B: Don't worry. He _____ fine. _____ he very excited this morning?
(be)   (Be)

A: No, but I _____ . I couldn't find my keys and I _____ the garbage in the
(be)   (put)

   refrigerator.

5. A: Today is Ron's birthday.

   B: How old _____ he?
                (be)

   A: Forty.

   B: _____ you and Ron _____ anything special?
                                (do)

   A: Yes. We _____ dinner with three couples tonight.
             (have)

VIII. Synthesis: Error Correction

Correct these sentences.

1. We going to take grandma to the doctor. <u>We're going to take grandma to the doctor.</u>

2. We'll be home last night. _____

3. When are we going see the doctor? _____

4. How we are going to get there by eleven o'clock? _____

   _____

5. Last year she's going to graduate from college. _____

   _____

6. May I to help you? _____

7. Who does he going to invite? _____

8. Just ask her and I'm sure she'll helps. _____

9. A week ago they're going to take a vacation. _____

   _____

10. Take your umbrella. It might rains. _____

Unit 11: Final Test

I. *Be Going to* for the Future: Affirmative and Negative Statements

*Complete the sentences with the affirmative or negative forms of **be going to** for the future. Use the words in parentheses.*

1. Dick lost his library card because he kept it in his pocket.

   (get a new one tomorrow) He *'s going to get a new one tomorrow.*_____

   (keep his new one in his pocket) He _____

2. I'm busy today. I'm working.

   (visit my aunt today) I _____

   (visit my aunt tomorrow) I _____

3. We don't have enough money to buy a new car.

   (buy a new car) We _____

   (buy a used car) We _____

4. Those carrots are a funny color, but the lettuce looks delicious.

   (buy any carrots) I _____

   (buy some lettuce) I _____

5. She's thirsty. She isn't hungry.

   (drink a glass of water) She _____

   (eat anything) She _____

II. Contrast: *Be Going to* for the Future and Simple Past

Complete the sentences with the correct form of the verb in parentheses. Use **be going to** *for the future or the simple past tense.*

1. They _____*met*_____ two months ago. He _____ her an
            (meet)   (give)

   engagement ring last month. Next month they _____ married.
                                                       (get)

2. She wants to live near her family. Last weekend she _____ for an apartment
                                                              (look)

   near her sister, but she _____ one. Next weekend she
                                 (find, not)

   _____ for an apartment near her brother.
         (look)

3. Last night we _____ to a concert in the park. We
    (go)

_____ some jazz music. We _____ it so much that
    (hear)   (enjoy)

next week we _____ back for another concert.
                   (go)

4. The video _____ due yesterday, but he _____ to
                 (be)   (forget)

return it. Since he _____ the movie on time, he
                          (return, not)

_____ a fine.
    (pay)

5. Last summer I _____ a vacation, but next summer I
                       (take not)

_____ a long vacation and visit several countries in Europe.
    (take)

III. Present Progressive for the Future

Complete the conversation with the correct form of the verb in parentheses.
Use the present progressive for the future.

A: Where ____are____ you ____going____ tomorrow?
                            1. (go)

B: We _____ to the mountains.
            2. (drive)

A: _____ you _____ there overnight?
                      3. (stay)

B: No. We _____ back after dinner. What about you?
                4. (drive)

A: I _____ to the beach with my cousin. We _____ at nine in the morning and
      5. (go)   6. (leave)

_____ late at night.
        7. (return)

IV. *Will* for the Future: Affirmative and Negative Statements

*Complete the conversations. Use the affirmative or negative of **will** and the*
words in parentheses.

1. A: My bracelet is broken.

   B: Give it to me. _____ I'll fix it. _____
                                    (I/fix/it)

2. A: I can't do this math problem.

   B: Ask Bob. _____
                      (He/explain/it/to you)

3. A: Why are you so angry at Billy?

   B: I prepared this delicious roast beef. _____

   (He/eat/it)

   He says he hates roast beef.

4. A: What is Scot going to buy you for your birthday?

   B: _____ He says it's a surprise.

   (He/tell/me)

5. A: I can't do all these dishes.

   B: _____

   (I/help/you)

   A: Thanks.

V. Contrast: *May/Might/Will*

Choose the correct word or words in parentheses to complete the conversations.

1. A: Is he going to stay at a hotel?

   B: I'm not sure. He ____might____ stay with friends.

   (might, 'll)

2. A: How long are you going to be away from the office?

   B: I _____ definitely be away for a week. I _____ even be away for two

   (may, 'll)   (might, 'll)

   weeks.

3. A: My suitcases are very heavy.

   B: I _____ help you carry them.

   (may, 'll)

4. A: Take an umbrella. The weatherman says it's going to rain.

   B: He doesn't know what he's talking about. It _____ rain. There isn't a cloud in the

   (may not, won't)

   sky.

5. A: Sometimes John goes to that restaurant. We _____ see him there.

   (may, 'll)

   B: I hope so.

Verb Tense Forms: Simple Present Tense, Present Progressive, Simple Past Tense,
VI. *Be Going to* for the Future, *Will* for the Future

Complete the sentences. Use the correct form of the following words in each sentence. In some cases there is more than one correct answer.

Janet/paint/a picture

1. Last night ___Janet painted a picture._____

2. At this moment _____

3. Is _____ now?

4. Does _____ every week?

5. Will _____ next week?

6. Is _____ tomorrow?

7. Last month _____ (not)

8. Next month _____ (not)

Simple Present Tense, Present Progressive, Simple Past Tense, *Be Going to*
VII. and *Will* for the Future

Complete the conversations. Use the correct form of the verb in parentheses.

1. A: Where _____is_____ Dan?
      (be)

   B: He _____ to the video store.
        (go)

   A: What _____ he _____ ?
                                 (get)

   B: He _____ to see *Casablanca*.
        (want)

   A: I hope it's there.

2. A: When _____ John _____ for college?
                              (leave)

   B: In two weeks.

   A: How _____ he _____ all his things to college?
                            (take)

   B: Bill and I _____ him there.
                 (drive)

   A: You _____ a truck.
          (need)

   B: _____ you _____ so?
                         (think)

3. A: What _____ you _____ to your hair? It's so curly.
         (do)

   B: I _____ a body wave. _____ you _____ it?
         (get)   (like)

   A: Yes. It _____ pretty.
             (be)

   B: Thanks. I _____ to a big party next Saturday night.
                 (go)

4. A: I _____ what to do. There _____ a leak in my bathroom.
        (know, not)   (be)

   B: Don't worry. I'm a plumber. I _____ it for you.
                                      (fix)

   A: Really?

   B: Really.

5. A. Hiro and Emiko _____ married next month, but it's a secret. Please don't tell any-
                      (get)

   one.

   B: Don't worry. I _____ anyone.
                      (tell, not)

VIII. Synthesis: Error Correction

Correct these sentences.

1. Who's going return the jacket? Who's going to return the jacket? _____

2. She might takes an art course. _____

3. When you going to study biology? _____

4. Last week there's going to be an art exhibit in the university library. _____

   _____

5. Will you to marry me? _____

6. He'll not wear his glasses. _____

7. How we getting to school today? _____

8. It may snows tonight. Don't forget your boots. _____

   _____

9. I'm going to doing the laundry. _____

10. How long they going to be away? _____

Unit 12: Diagnostic Test

I. Comparative Form of Adjectives

Write comparative sentences. Use the words in parentheses.

1. (an armchair/comfortable/a bench)

   An armchair is more comfortable than a bench. _____

2. (car/expensive/a bicycle)

   _____

3. (a mountain/high/a hill)

   _____

4. (an ocean/big/a river)

   _____

II. Adjectives and Adverbs

Choose the correct word in parentheses to complete each sentence.

1. She sings _____ well _____ .
   (good, well)
2. We have a _____ violin.
   (good, well)
3. She eats _____ .
   (slow, slowly)
4. We're studying for a test. Please speak _____ .
   (soft, softly)
5. They work _____ .
   (hard, hardly)
6. They are _____ workers.
   (hard, hardly)
7. When will I speak English _____ ?
   (fluent, fluently)
8. He's a very _____ driver.
   (careful, carefully)
9. I have a _____ cold.
   (bad, badly)
10. He did _____ on the test.
    (bad, badly)

III. Comparative Form of Adverbs

Write comparative questions. Use the words in parentheses.

1. (dogs/live long/cats)

   Do dogs live longer than cats?

2. (men/eat fast/women)

   _____

3. (men/drive carefully/women)

   _____

4. (doctors/work hard/nurses)

   _____

IV. *Too/Very*

*Complete the sentences. Use **too** or **very**.*

1. He can't get a driver's license. He's _____too_____ young.

2. Wear light clothes. It's _____ hot outside.

3. My son grew three inches. Now all his pants are _____ short for him to wear.

4. I'm _____ tired to watch that movie. I'm going to sleep.

V. Comparisons: the Comparative, the Same, Different, and Equal

*Complete the sentences. Use **as, from, than**.*

1. I have the same initials ____as____ my brother.

2. My ideas are very different _____ my parents'.

3. Today her cold is worse _____ it was yesterday.

4. They aren't as poor _____ they say.

5. My umbrella is the same _____ yours.

6. She is more industrious _____ her sister.

7. The movie is less expensive _____ the play.

8. The second edition is different _____ the first edition.

VI. *More/Less/Fewer* + Nouns

Complete the sentences. Use **more, less,** *or* **fewer.**

1. We couldn't finish on time. The job took _____more_____ time than we expected.

2. We were lucky. There were _____ problems than before.

3. A word processor costs _____ money than a computer.

4. There were twenty students in my class last semester. This semester there are fifteen. There are

   _____ students this semester.

5. I can't see well here. I need _____ light.

6. This vegetable soup has no taste. Next time use _____ water and more vegetables.

VII. Comparisons

Choose the correct words to complete each sentence.

1. Dino doesn't speak Spanish as _____*well as*_____ Norma does.
   - a. well as
   - b. good as
   - c. better than

2. A Cadillac is _____ a Subaru.
   - a. bigger than
   - b. big as
   - c. more than big

3. A Cadillac is _____ than a Subaru.
   - a. as expensive
   - b. most expensive
   - c. more expensive

4. He often comes to school _____.
   - a. late
   - b. lately
   - c. more late

5. He works _____.
   - a. quick
   - b. quickly
   - c. as quicker

6. Elenore drives more _____ Pete.
   - a. carefully than
   - b. careful than
   - c. careful as

7. His cold is _____ today than it was yesterday.
   a. bad
   b. worse
   c. badly

8. He isn't _____ to go to kindergarten.
   a. enough old
   b. old enough
   c. older enough

9. We aren't _____ we think.
   a. as important as
   b. important as
   c. more important as

VIII. Synthesis: Error Correction

Correct these sentences.

1. He hired less workers than before. He hired fewer workers than before. _____

2. He's enough strong to be a weight lifter. _____

3. An elephant is more bigger than a dog. _____

4. She writes good. _____

5. My sister is very different my brother. _____

6. Are you as older as your cousin? _____

7. There were less people than last year. _____

8. This is a comfortabler chair than the other chair. _____

   _____

9. That's a too nice tie. _____

10. She has a busy schedule than he does. _____

Unit 12: Final Test

I. Comparative Form of Adjectives

Write comparative sentences. Use the words in parentheses.

1. (an elephant/big/a mouse) An elephant is bigger than a mouse.

2. (a rabbit/fast/a turtle) _____

3. (a diamond/expensive/a pearl) _____

4. (a fur jacket/warm/a jeans jacket) _____

II. Adjectives and Adverbs

Choose the correct word in parentheses to complete each sentence.

1. This peach tastes _____good_____ .
   (good, well)
2. He works _____ .
   (slow, slowly)
3. She never hides her feelings. She speaks _____ .
   (open, openly)
4. He always gets up _____ on the weekend.
   (late, lately)
5. Let him drive. He drives _____ .
   (careful, carefully)
6. She's a very _____ lawyer. I'd like her to work for me.
   (clever, cleverly)
7. The food at that restaurant is very _____ .
   (bad, badly)
8. Don't be afraid. My dog is _____ .
   (friend, friendly)
9. She answered _____ .
   (quick, quickly)
10. Does he take _____ messages?
    (accurate, accurately)

III. Comparative Form of Adverbs

Write comparative questions. Use the words in parentheses.

1. (men/live long/women) Do men live longer than women?

2. (men/drive slowly/women) _____

3. (lions/run fast/tigers) _____

4. (fried chicken/taste good/broiled chicken) _____

IV. *Too/Very*

Complete the sentences. Use **too** *or* **very**.

1. This is a _____*very*_____ important letter. Please make sure there aren't any mistakes in it.

2. He's _____ young to be the president.

3. She's _____ strong. She goes to a gym and works out every day.

4. I can't wear those shoes. My feet are _____ big.

V. Comparisons: the Comparative, the Same, Different, and Equal

Complete the sentences. Use **as, from,** *or* **than**.

1. Is he as talented _____*as*_____ his brother?

2. These new mops are very different _____ the old ones.

3. His eyes are bigger _____ his stomach.

4. The bus is less expensive _____ the train.

5. My science course isn't as difficult _____ my math course.

6. I have the same expenses _____ she does.

7. She is more confident now _____ she was in the past.

8. He had better references _____ the other man.

VI. *More/Less/Fewer* + Nouns

Complete the sentences. Use **more, less,** *or* **fewer**.

1. His life is a mess. He's rich, but he has _____*more*_____ problems than he had when he was poor.

2. Many students didn't return this year. There are _____ students now than there were before.

3. In the summer many businesses are closed, so we get _____ mail than at other times of the year.

4. My history paper has fifty footnotes. My English paper has thirty footnotes. My English paper has _____ footnotes than my history paper.

5. I can't finish this test. I need ——————— time.

6. You're drowning that plant. Use ——————— water.

VII. Comparisons

Choose the correct words to complete each sentence.

1. My son is _____ old enough _____ to vote.
   - a. enough old
   - b. older enough
   - c. old enough

2. My secretary types very _____ .
   - a. accurately
   - b. more accurate
   - c. accurate

3. The food in our dormitory tastes as _____ it looks.
   - a. worse as
   - b. badly as
   - c. bad as

4. Are bears _____ lions?
   - a. heavier than
   - b. more heavy than
   - c. heavier

5. She drives _____ he does.
   - a. more fast than
   - b. faster than
   - c. more faster than

6. Is that bookcase _____ for all your books?
   - a. big enough
   - b. enough big
   - c. as big

7. The Browns are _____ their neighbors.
   - a. more generous than
   - b. generous than
   - c. as generous than

8. He sleeps much _____ at home than he did in the hospital.
   - a. good
   - b. more good
   - c. better

VIII. Synthesis: Error Correction

Correct these sentences.

1. We sold less pictures than before. <u>We sold fewer pictures than before.</u>

2. There's fewer homework today so we have time to study for the test. _____

3. Are you enough experienced to be the director? _____

4. Does he work as quickly his partner does? _____

5. Is it as late than I think? _____

6. Is the bracelet more expensive the earrings? _____

7. He works more harder than his boss does. _____

8. She sings very good. _____

9. That's a too beautiful vest. _____

10. Today's news is worse yesterday's news. _____

Unit 13: Diagnostic Test

I. Past Progressive and Simple Past Tense

Complete the sentences. Use the correct form of the past progressive or the simple past tense.

1. We _____ were watching _____ TV last night when a friend from Australia
   _____(watch)_____
   _____ called _____ .
   _____(call)_____

2. When the doorbell _____ , I _____ a shower.
   _____(ring)_____ _____(take)_____

3. He _____ when he _____ and
   _____(ski)_____ _____(fall)_____
   _____ his ankle.
   _____(break)_____

4. They _____ when a bird _____ in the open window.
   _____(sleep)_____ _____(fly)_____

5. _____ you _____ when you
   _____(shave)_____
   _____ your chin?
   _____(cut)_____

6. When the doorbell _____ , I _____ and
   _____(ring)_____ _____(run)_____
   _____ it.
   _____(answer)_____

II. Direct and Indirect Objects

*Complete the conversations. Use **to** or **for**.*

1. A: Why did you send John a T-shirt?

   B: I sent it _____ to _____ him for his birthday.

2. A: Yoko, is this Japanese?

   B: Yes, it is.

   A: Would you translate it _____ me?

   B: Sure. No problem.

3. A: Did you make a card _____ him?

   B: Yes, and I sent it _____ him last Thursday.

4. A: When did you lend the car _____ your son?

   B: This morning at eleven o'clock.

5. A: He didn't believe me at first, but then I proved it —————— him.

   B: That's good.

6. A: Could you fix this lamp —————— me?

   B: No, I'm sorry. I don't know anything about electricity.

III. Object Pronouns with Direct and Indirect Objects

Rewrite these sentences. Change the underlined word or words to **it** *or* **them**.

1. She found the <u>the dictionary</u> for her son.

   She found it for her son.
   _____

2. They gave <u>a lot of money</u> to that hospital.

   _____

3. She read the children <u>the folk tales</u>.

   _____

4. We built <u>this dog house</u> for our dog.

   _____

5. I showed my friends <u>my drawings</u>.

   _____

6. He told the judge <u>the story</u>.

   _____

IV. *Too/Either*

Complete the conversations. Write a short response with **too** *or* **either**.

1. A: I saw that film.

   B: I _____ *did too* _____ .

2. A: We're going to get a VCR.

   B: We _____ .

3. A: I didn't pay my phone bill.

   B: I _____ .

4. A: I can't ski.

   B: I _____ .

5. A: She isn't a teacher.

   B: He _____ .

6. A: We won't leave.

   B: They _____ .

7. A: I'd like to visit New Zealand.

   B: I _____ .

V. Phrasal Verbs with Direct Objects

Complete the sentences. Use **in, off,** *or* **back.**

1. It was hot so all the men took their jackets ___off___ .

2. You really need to have a meeting with her. Don't put it _____ again.

3. It's twelve o'clock. Please hand your tests _____ now.

4. It was cold, so I borrowed my friend's sweater last night. I don't want to forget to give it _____ today.

5. It's cool outside. We don't need the air conditioner. I'm going to turn it _____ .

VI. Phrasal Verbs without Direct Objects

Complete the conversations. Use the correct form of the phrasal verbs in the box.

| break down | catch on | grow up |
| come in | clear up | |

1. A: Oh, John. I'm so happy to see you. Please ___come in___ and stay for a while.

   B: Thanks.

2. A: What are you doing?

   B: I'm calling my mechanic. My car _____ and I need to get it fixed quickly.

3. A: That new worker is wonderful. He _____ to everything very quickly.

   B: He seems very bright to me, too.

4. A: It's foggy now, but it will probably _____ later.

   B: I hope so.

5. A: They really hate the city. They both _____ in the country and want to

   move back to the country as soon as possible.

   B: I wish them luck.

VII. Synthesis: Error Correction

Correct these sentences.

1. He ice skated when he broke his ankle. *He was ice skating when he broke his ankle.*

2. I didn't do my homework and my friend didn't, too. _____

   _____

3. We were driving across the bridge when our car broke out. _____

   _____

4. Would you explain me that sentence? _____

5. She sent to me a box of cookies. _____

6. We was listening to the radio when we heard about that accident. _____

   _____

7. Please don't leave your clothes on the chair. Hang them. _____

   _____

8. Would you please throw away them. _____

9. Give it me. _____

10. Why was you standing in the rain? _____

Unit 13: Final Test

I. Past Progressive and Simple Past Tense

Complete the sentences. Use the correct form of the past progressive or the simple past tense.

1. I _____was walking_____ along the street when I _____ a beautiful
   (walk)   (see)
   orange and black butterfly.

2. When I _____ home, the children _____ a cake.
   (come)   (bake)

3. He _____ golf with his boss when he _____ a hole in
   (play)   (get)
   one.

4. Unfortunately he _____ when he cut his face.
   (shave)

5. They _____ home from work when they _____ the
   (drive)   (hear)
   news on their car radio.

6. First I _____ breakfast. Then I _____ to the post
   (eat)   (drive)
   office.

II. Direct and Indirect Objects

*Complete the conversations. Use **to** or **for**.*

1. A: Everyone liked my short story.

   B: How do you know?

   A: The teacher read it ____to____ the class.

2. A: Why are you giving him fifty dollars?

   B: I owe it _____ him.

3. A: What is the government doing with that money?

   B: Building a home _____ senior citizens.

4. A: I need some money. Could you cash a check _____ me?

   B: Certainly.

5. A: Would you pronounce the word *antique* _____ me?

   B: It's pronounced /æn´tiᵏk/.

   A: Thanks.

6. A: Did you find your glasses?

   B: No. Lenore found them _____ me.

III. Object Pronouns with Direct and Indirect Objects

Rewrite the sentences. Change the underlined word or words to **it** *or* **them**.

1. I gave my friend <u>a basket of fruit</u>. *I gave it to my friend.* _____

2. She showed us <u>her new photos</u>. _____

3. We bought <u>a watch</u> for our son. _____

4. They told their parents <u>a lie</u>. _____

5. He made <u>dinner</u> for me. _____

6. I owe the bank <u>a lot of money</u>. _____

IV. *Too/Either*

Complete the conversations. Write a short response. Use **too** *or* **either**.

1. A: You ate hot dogs.

   B: You _____ *did too* _____ .

2. A: She lives near the beach.

   B: Her friend _____ .

3. A: We're going to pick blueberries.

   B: They _____ .

4. A: I'm not studying anymore.

   B: I _____ .

5. A: We weren't sleeping at 10:00 P.M.

   B: They _____ .

6. A: We can understand a little Greek.

   B: Bill _____ .

7. A: He didn't pass the test.

   B: She _____ .

V. Phrasal Verbs with Direct Objects

*Complete the sentences. Use **away, on,** or **up**.*

1. I really need those magazines. Please don't throw them ___away___ .

2. I can't hear what the reporter is saying. It's too low. Turn the volume _____ .

3. She put _____ a big hat and sunglasses, and nobody recognized her.

4. Put your books _____ . They don't belong on the floor.

5. I'm wrapping _____ all the presents.

VI. Phrasal Verbs without Direct Objects

Complete the conversations. Use the correct form of the phrasal verbs in the box.

eat out	break down	stand up
hang up	come up	

1. A: I called you all evening. You weren't at home.

   B: We ___ate out___ and went to a concert in the park.

2. A: Who was that?

   B: I don't know. When I picked up the phone, the person on the other end

   _____ .

3. A: When the president entered, everyone _____ and applauded.

   B: How exciting!

4. A: The computers at the bank are terrible. They _____ every other week.

   B: I know.

5. A: When did that problem _____ ?

   B: During the general meeting.

VII. Synthesis: Error Correction

Correct these sentences.

1. He worked in the garden when the dog bit him. <u>He was working in the garden when the dog</u> <u>bit him.</u>

2. He doesn't speak Turkish and his wife doesn't, too. _____

_____

3. He can't explain me that joke. _____

4. Who were stand on the roof? _____

5. He's a good cook, but he doesn't like to cook. He prefers to eat up. _____

_____

6. I found a good carpenter to you. _____

7. He gave him it. _____

8. What was you doing last night at eleven o'clock? _____

_____

9. I talked on the telephone when the doorbell rang. _____

_____

10. I like fish and he likes, too. _____

Unit 14: Diagnostic Test

I. *Should:* Affirmative and Negative Statements

Complete the sentences. Use **should** *or* **shouldn't**.

1. We ___*should*___ eat a big breakfast before we leave. There aren't any good restaurants on the

    way, and we'll be on the road for many hours.

2. Those pants really don't fit him well. He _____ wear them for his job interview.

3. He has a bad cough. He _____ stay home and rest. He _____ go to the

    party.

4. You _____ turn off the lights before you leave. Electricity costs a lot of money.

II. *Had better:* Affirmative and Negative Statements

Complete the sentences. Use **'d better** *or* **'d better not**.

1. You ___*'d better*___ buy a few more bottles of soda. We'll need them for the party

    tonight.

2. He _____ say that again. It was a terrible thing to say.

3. It's raining. You _____ take an umbrella.

4. You _____ call before you visit. They may not be home.

III. *Have to/Must:* Affirmative and Negative Statements

Complete the sentences. Use the affirmative or negative of **have to, has to,** *or*
must.

1. It's dangerous to climb those rocks. Tell the children they ___*mustn't*___ climb them.

2. It's okay to wear jeans to the party. You _____ wear a suit and tie.

3. He can't go to the movies. He _____ study for a test.

4. She _____ take the test. She can write a report instead.

5. He can't go to the party. He _____ take care of his younger brother.

IV. *Have to:* Present and Past

Complete the sentences. Use **have to, has to,** *or* **had to**.

1. Last week we ___*had to*___ work late every day.

2. She doesn't have a good dictionary. She _____ buy one.

3. It was a good movie, but we —————————— wait in line for an hour to get tickets.

4. Nobody gave him his car. He —————————— work for it.

5. We can't use a check. We —————————— pay by cash.

V. Modal Review

Choose the correct word or words in parentheses to complete the conversations.

1. A: I have a problem. What _____ should _____ I do? My boss wants me to work this
   (would, should, may)
   Sunday at the same time as my son is going to be in a school play.

   B: See your son's play.

2. A: How _____ I reach you in an emergency?
   (must, can, may)
   B: Call my secretary at 738-2900. She can always find me.

3. A: You _____ say anything bad about my family.
   ('d better not, couldn't, might not)
   B: Don't worry. I won't.

4. A: _____ you like to see my photos?
   (Could, Would, Should)
   B: Are they photos of your last trip?

5. A: She _____ to drink more juice.
   (ought, had better, should)
   B: Why?

6. A: We can write our compositions by hand. We _____ use a word processor
   (couldn't, wouldn't, don't have to)
   or computer.

   B: That's good.

VI. Superlative Form of Adjectives and Adverbs

Complete the sentences. Use the superlative form of the words in parentheses.

1. He is one of _____ the greatest _____ men in history.
   (great)
2. The Mississippi River is _____ river in the United States.
   (long)
3. She earns _____ salary in the company.
   (high)
4. Is Russia _____ country in the world?
   (big)
5. Tokyo is one of _____ cities in the world.
   (expensive)

6. Football is one of _____ sports in our high school.
   (dangerous)
7. She arrived _____ of all.
   (early)
8. Tuesday is _____ day of the week.
   (busy)

VII. Contrast: Superlative and Comparative Forms

Complete the sentences. Use the superlative or comparative forms of the words in parentheses.

1. Is Bob _____ the youngest _____ one in his family?
   (young)
2. Who wrote _____ composition of all?
   (good)
3. The new buses are _____ the old ones.
   (bad)
4. Is the written report _____ the oral one?
   (important)
5. She is _____ one in her class.
   (friendly)
6. My mother is _____ my father.
   (generous)
7. June is usually _____ May.
   (warm)
8. Dan is _____ man in the world.
   (handsome)

VIII. Synthesis: Error Correction

Correct these sentences.

1. Is Joan the most tall one in her office? Is Joan the tallest one in her office? _____

2. She'd better to walk to work. _____

3. It isn't safe to stand in the rowboat. You mustn't to stand in it. _____

   _____

4. What should we takes to the beach? _____

5. Last week we must work until 10:00 P.M. _____

6. He is one of the most industrious worker in the company. _____

   _____

7. He ought to gets new front tires. _____

8. Next week she had to go to the dentist. _____

9. You'd better not to leave your ring in the bathroom. _____

_____

10. Who is the more experienced secretary of the three? _____

_____

Unit 14: Final Test

I. *Should:* Affirmative and Negative Statements

Complete the sentences. Use **should** *or* **shouldn't**.

1. She seems lonely. We _____*should*_____ visit her.

2. We all like those donuts, but they have a lot of fat in them. You _____ buy them.

3. You really _____ complain all the time. It makes everyone feel bad.

4. I have a problem with my visa. Where _____ I go for help?

II. *Had better:* Affirmative and Negative Statements

Complete the sentences. Use **'d better** *or* **'d better not**.

1. We _____*'d better*_____ bring those chairs inside. I think it's going to rain.

2. They _____ ask for more money. We gave them fifty dollars last week and

   forty the week before.

3. You _____ finish the bread. We need some for tomorrow.

4. You _____ write me a memo. Otherwise I may forget.

III. *Have to/Must:* Affirmative and Negative Statements

Complete the sentences. Use the affirmative or negative of **have to, has to,** *or*
must.

1. When do you _____*have to*_____ go back to the dentist?

2. She _____ pay that bill before the first of the month.

3. Be very careful. There are many cars on that street. You _____ cross when the light is

   red.

4. She's lucky. She can come to the office any time before eleven. She _____ come at nine

   o'clock like the rest of us.

5. Our homework is due tomorrow. We _____ hand it in today.

IV. *Have to:* Present and Past

Complete the sentences. Use **have to, has to,** *or* **had to**.

1. Two years ago they _____*had to*_____ work seven days a week. Now that their business is success-

   ful, they only work five days a week.

2. To get a high school diploma, you _____ study a second language.

3. When I was a child, I _____ practice the piano an hour every day.

4. She can't go to the concert. She _____ work.

5. He couldn't read the message. He _____ ask someone to read it for him.

V. Modal Review

Choose the correct word or words in parentheses to complete the conversations.

1. A: _____ Would _____ you like to see my boat?
     (Could, Would, Should)
   B: Certainly.

2. A: What will you do after dinner?

   B: We're not sure. We _____ take a walk or we _____
                        (might, should, will)   (might, should, will)
   see a movie.

3. A: Everyone talks about that play. We _____ to get tickets for it.
                                          (ought, should, 'd better)
   B: You're right.

4. A: You can wear whatever you want. You _____ wear dress clothes.
                                          (mustn't, don't have to, may not)

5. The animals are dangerous. He really _____ feed them.
                                         (doesn't have to, mustn't, wouldn't)

6. You _____ worry. There's nothing you can do to change things.
      (couldn't, mightn't, shouldn't)

VI. Superlative Form of Adjectives and Adverbs

Complete the sentences. Use the superlative form of the words in parentheses.

1. The Sears Tower in Chicago is _____ the tallest _____ building in the United States.
                                 (tall)

2. She types _____ of all the secretaries.
            (accurately)

3. Switerzland is one of _____ countries in the world.
                         (beautiful)

4. Rhode Island is _____ state in the United States.
                   (small)

5. Who is _____ student in the class?
          (funny)

6. He ran _____ of all.
          (fast)

7. New York City is one of _____ cities in the world.
                           (important)

8. He chose _____ gift he could find.
            (cheap)

VII. Contrast: Superlative and Comparative Forms

Complete the sentences. Use the superlative or comparative forms of the words in parentheses.

1. The older man works _____harder than_____ than the younger one.
   (hard)
2. Is the diamond _____ stone in the world?
   (hard)
3. We had _____ time of our lives.
   (good)
4. My new bed is _____ my old one.
   (comfortable)
5. February is one of _____ months of the year.
   (cold)
6. Is February _____ March?
   (cold)
7. I usually get up _____ my husband does.
   (early)
8. What's _____ way to get to the post office from here?
   (fast)

VIII. Synthesis: Error Correction

Correct these sentences.

1. You better not forget your report. _You'd better not forget your report.___

2. He is the most tall one in the class. _____

3. They shouldn't to complain so much. _____

4. Last month I have to take three important tests. _____

   _____

5. She ought to spends less money. _____

6. That is one of the most important discovery of the century. _____

   _____

7. That pot is very hot. You might not touch it. _____

8. Does she has to work all summer? _____

9. Thanksgiving is one of the important holidays of the year. _____

   _____

10. I want her to drive. She drives the more carefully of all. _____

    _____